SIXTH EDITION

HARBRACE WORKBOOK FOR CANADIANS

SIXTH EDITION

HARBRACE WORKBOOK FOR CANADIANS

alia Canada Mexico Singapore Spain United Kingdom United States

Harbrace Workbook for Canadians
Sixth Edition

By William Connor

Editorial Director and Publisher:
Evelyn Veitch

Acquisitions Editor:
Anne Williams

Marketing Manager:
Cara Yarzab

Senior Developmental Editor:
Rebecca Rea

Production Editor:
Carrie Withers

Senior Production Coordinator:
Hedy Sellers

Copy Editor and Proofreader:
Rohini Herbert

Creative Director:
Angela Cluer

Cover Design:
Ken Phipps

Compositor:
Erich Falkenberg

Printer:
Transcontinental

Printed and bound in Canada
7 8 09 08

For more information contact Nelson, 1120 Birchmount Road, Scarborough, Ontario, M1K 5G4. Or you can visit our Internet site at http://www.nelson.com

ISBN-13: 978-0-17-622510-0
ISBN-10: 0-17-622510-2

National Library of Canada Cataloguing in Publication Data

Connor, William
Harbrace workbook for Canadians/William Connor.

ISBN 0-17-622510-2

1. English language—Grammar
Problems, exercises, etc.
2. English language—Rhetoric—
Problems, exercises, etc.
I. Title

PE1112.H615 2003 808'042
C2002-905644-6

Preface

The exercises in the *Harbrace Workbook for Canadians*, Sixth Edition, are designed to reinforce the explanations in the *Harbrace Handbook for Canadians*, Sixth Edition, by providing students with practice and a means of testing their understanding. To avoid confusion and minimize waste, the *Workbook* relies on the explanations provided in the *Handbook* and repeats only the main points of advice. The directions provided with the exercises and the explanations in the *Handbook* will allow students to handle most chapters with little guidance, but where effective writing, rather than correctness, is the main concern, acceptable answers may vary from the sample corrections provided, and some students may need help in judging the quality of their responses. Even with these chapters, however, students should be encouraged to work independently so that classroom time and individual help may be devoted to more advanced matters. The extent to which the *Workbook* is used in the classroom will, of course, depend on the level of the students being taught and on the degree to which the *Handbook* is used as a teaching text or a reference book. However, it should be stressed that doing exercises is no substitute for writing itself and that the *Workbook* is intended not as a substitute for writing but as an efficient means of solving problems that make writing difficult and diminish its effectiveness.

The basic pattern for using the workbook is the same throughout: Read the chapter in the *Handbook*. Do an exercise without checking the answers until the exercise is complete. Check the answers to evaluate success. Follow the directions accompanying the exercise to find out whether to proceed to the next exercise or to review relevant material in the *Handbook* before going on. The *Workbook* can be used effectively for either remedial review related to specific problems or as reinforcement for material that is being studied in the *Handbook*.

Publisher's Note to Instructors and Students

Thank you for selecting the *Harbrace Workbook for Canadians*, Sixth Edition, by William Connor. The author and publisher have devoted considerable time to the careful development of this book, and we appreciate your recognition of this effort and accomplishment.

We want to hear what you think about the *Harbrace Workbook for Canadians*. Please take a few minutes to fill out the stamped reply card at the back of the book. Your comments, suggestions, and criticisms will be valuable to us as we prepare new editions and other books.

Contents

GRAMMAR

1 Sentence Sense

An English sentence can be divided into two parts: the subject (what the sentence is about) and the predicate (which says something about the subject).

1a
Verbs form the predicates of sentences.

1b
Subjects, objects, and complements can be nouns, pronouns, or word groups serving as nouns.

A predicate is the part of a sentence comprising what is said about the subject. The complete predicate consists of the main verb and its auxiliaries (the simple predicate) and any complements and modifiers. The subject is a noun or noun substitute about which something is asserted or asked in the predicate. The complete subject consists of the simple subject and the words associated with it.

■ Exercise 1.1
In each of the following sentences, the simple subject of a clause appears in boldfaced type. Underline the verb (including any auxiliaries) that relates to this subject. Check your answers on page 121. If you make more than one mistake, review section **1a** of the *Handbook* before going on to the next exercise.

1. Coming from Toronto, **Asha** was surprised by the variety and number of waterfowl living in the lakes of Western Canada.
2. We could not decide whether the **stars** in a boxlike configuration were part of the Draco or Ursa Minor constellation.
3. The **Canadian Shield** was the first part of North America to rise permanently above sea level.
4. **Igor** strode up to the witness stand, raised his right hand, swore to tell the whole truth, and looked the prosecuting attorney straight in the eye.
5. Some **insurers** will substantially reduce the amount you pay for life insurance if you have never been a cigarette smoker.
6. The best smoke alarms are the ones that warn you when their **batteries** become weak.
7. The **books** in the library were deteriorating rapidly because of the excessive humidity.

8. My present **job** is boring and pays poorly, so I intend to apply to an M.B.A. program as soon as possible.
9. Will **you** stay for dinner?
10. **I** have sometimes encountered snow in the Quebec woods in July.

■ Exercise 1.2

In each of the following sentences, a verb appears in boldfaced type. Underline the simple subjects of these verbs. Check your answers on page 121. If you make more than one mistake, review section **1b** of the *Handbook* before going on to the next exercise.

1. There **is** statistical evidence that seat belts save lives.
2. Few Canadians realize that the highest area in the country between the mountains of Labrador and the Rockies **is** Cypress Hills Provincial Park in southwestern Saskatchewan.
3. The hills **were** apparently **created** by the huge glaciers of the Ice Age.
4. Only of spiders **was** Bart really **frightened**.
5. **Will** you **visit** Vancouver and Victoria again this summer?
6. In the lot behind the warehouse **were** several abandoned cars.
7. The villain of *Hamlet* **is** Claudius.
8. Tied to the wharf, the sailboat in which Captain LeBlanc had crossed the Atlantic **looked** small and fragile.
9. The birds, as well as the bees, **fly** and **lay** eggs.
10. Twenty cheerleaders, even without the basketball team itself, **can be** a handful on a school bus meant for forty.

■ Exercise 1.3

In each of the following sentences, a verb appears in boldfaced type. In the parentheses that follow the sentence, the element you are to underline is specified: the direct or indirect object of the boldfaced verb or the subject or object complement in the clause in which this verb appears. Check your answers on page 121. If you make more than one mistake, review section **1b** of the *Handbook* before going on to the next exercise.

1. The volcanoes of Mexico **provide** climbers with experience at high altitude. (indirect object)
2. Many peaks in the Canadian Rockies **are** far more challenging technically than Mexico's volcanoes. (subject complement)
3. Everyone **helped** the victims at the accident scene. (direct object)

4. Considering the figures objectively, one **must admit** that the chances of being attacked by a bear are far slimmer than the chances of being involved in a car accident on the way to the park. (direct object)
5. Gino **bought** his grandfather a new car with his lottery winnings. (indirect object)
6. Admissions to some graduate schools **may be** closed by the time your fourth-year marks are available. (subject complement)
7. A short side trip north from the Trans-Canada Highway to old Route 132 **will be** worthwhile if you are driving through the Lower St. Lawrence. (subject complement)
8. Hiroko and Saito **called** their new baby Toshihiko. (object complement)
9. They **called** their first Ildiko. (direct object)
10. The class **elected** Mandy editor of the newsletter. (object complement)

■ Exercise 1.4

In each of the following sentences, a verb appears in boldfaced type. In the parentheses that follow the sentence, the element you are to underline is specified: the direct or indirect object of the boldfaced verb or the subject or object complement in the clause in which this verb appears. Check your answers on page 121. If you make more than one mistake, review section **1b** of the *Handbook* thoroughly before going on to the next exercise.

1. His testimony **seemed** reliable even though it had been several years since he had witnessed the incident. (subject complement)
2. Being on a diet, I **ordered** only soup, salad, and ice water. (direct object)
3. The gallery **offers** visitors a remarkable collection of Oriental painting and sculpture comparable to any other collection on the continent. (indirect object)
4. The children **made** Yuri's visiting cousin's pet parrot an honorary member of their club, but they made the bird take the traditional oath of secrecy. (object complement)
5. The parrot **was** faithful to his oath and spoke only of crackers and things obscene. (subject complement)
6. The *Times* **stores** its archives on microfilm in a fireproof vault. (direct object)
7. Athens, Greece, **was** the site of the first Olympic Games in 1896. (subject complement)
8. Jack **gave** his mother the magic beans. (indirect object)

9. I **consider** a street guide indispensable for anyone who expects to drive in an unfamiliar city. (object complement)
10. The lobster **tasted** superb, but my boyfriend grumbled about not being able to order a hamburger. (subject complement)

1c
There are eight classes of words—the parts of speech.

The eight parts of speech are **verbs**, **nouns**, **pronouns**, **adjectives**, **adverbs**, **prepositions**, **conjunctions**, and **interjections**.

■ Exercise 1.5

In the blank to the right of each word, indicate which part of speech the word is in the sentence below. Check your answers on pages 121–22. If you make one mistake, be sure you understand your error. If you make more than one mistake, review section **1c** of the *Handbook* before going on to the next exercise.

Jameel hugged his knapsack in his sleep as the temperature in the old cabin dropped steadily.

1. Jameel ______________
2. hugged ______________
3. his ______________
4. knapsack ______________
5. in ______________
6. his ______________
7. sleep ______________
8. as ______________
9. the ______________
10. temperature ______________
11. in ______________
12. the ______________
13. old ______________
14. cabin ______________
15. dropped ______________
16. steadily ______________

■ Exercise 1.6

In the blank to the right of each word, indicate which part of speech the word is in the sentence below. Check your answers on page 122. If you make one mistake, be sure you understand your mistake before going on to the next exercise. If you make more than one mistake, review section **1c** of the *Handbook*.

Soon after graduation, Jacqueline found a job and began perfecting the skills she had acquired during her program.

1. Soon ____________________
2. after ____________________
3. graduation ____________________
4. Jacqueline ____________________
5. found ____________________
6. a ____________________
7. job ____________________
8. and ____________________
9. began ____________________
10. perfecting ____________________
11. the ____________________
12. skills ____________________
13. she ____________________
14. had ____________________
15. acquired ____________________
16. during ____________________
17. her ____________________
18. program ____________________

1d

A phrase is a group of words that functions as a single part of speech.

A phrase can function as a noun, a verb, an adjective, or an adverb. Phrases do not have subjects or predicates.

1e

Recognizing clauses helps in analyzing sentences.

A clause has both a subject and a predicate and functions as either an independent unit (*independent clause*) or a dependent unit (*subordinate clause*, used as an adverb, an adjective, or a noun).

■ Exercise 1.7

In the first blank following each of the sentences below, indicate whether the group of words underlined is a phrase or a subordinate clause. In the second blank, indicate which part of speech the phrase or clause functions as in its sentence. Check your answers on page 122. If you get nine out of ten right, make sure you understand your mistake before going on to the next exercise. If you make more than one mistake, review sections **1d** and **1e** of the *Handbook*.

1. My first daughter, Mei-Ling, was born on October 15, 1996.

   ____________________ ____________________

2. The man who will deliver the lecture on stress in the workplace has already had an ulcer and a mild heart attack.

   ____________________ ____________________

3. We will have to meet with the representatives from the shipping department after the Christmas rush is over.

   ____________________ ____________________

4. Anton's lifelong interest in music began when he was a choirboy.

   ____________________ ____________________

5. The security guard explained politely that the arena would not be open for another twenty minutes.

   ____________________ ____________________

6. The dancers in the chorus line were able to learn their new routines quickly.

   ____________________ ____________________

7. They have numerous pictures of Aaron getting his first haircut.

   ____________________ ____________________

8. They have numerous pictures of Aaron getting his first haircut.

   ____________________ ____________________

9. If we both go to the conference, we can save on expenses by sharing a room.

   ____________________ ____________________

10. If we both go to the conference, we can save on expenses by sharing a room.

    ____________________ ____________________

■ Exercise 1.8

In the first blank following each of the sentences below, indicate whether the group of words underlined is a phrase or a subordinate clause. In the second blank, indicate which part of speech the phrase or clause functions as in its sentence. Check your answers on page 122. If you get nine out of ten right, make sure you understand your mistake before going on to the next exercise. If you make more than one mistake, review sections **1d** and **1e** of the *Handbook*.

1. Most <u>of the students</u>, notwithstanding higher tuition fees and fewer summer jobs, hope to return to university in the fall.

   ______________ ______________

2. Who would like to volunteer <u>before all the jobs are taken</u>?

   ______________ ______________

3. <u>Because we were going skiing</u>, we had to skip the skating party.

   ______________ ______________

4. Where are you calling from <u>at this time of night</u>?

   ______________ ______________

5. <u>To sell</u> her most valued possession, an autographed copy of *Sunshine Sketches* by Stephen Leacock, would be a regrettable sacrifice.

   ______________ ______________

6. Are the Robitailles taking their children along <u>when they go to Florida this winter</u>?

   ______________ ______________

7. You will never be able to guess who the new owners <u>of the house</u> on the corner are.

   ______________ ______________

8. You will never be able to guess who the new owners of the house <u>on the corner</u> are.

   ______________ ______________

9. <u>Locked safely in a bank vault</u>, the deed to the property is registered in my name.

   ______________ ______________

10. Before <u>going out</u>, we always make sure the baby-sitter knows where to call if something goes wrong.

    ______________ ______________

1f

Sentences may be analyzed by form and function.

Learn to recognize main clauses and the various types of sentences. A **simple sentence** consists of a single independent clause. A **compound sentence** consists of at least two independent clauses and no subordinate clauses. A **complex sentence** has one independent clause and at least one subordinate clause. A **compound-complex sentence** consists of at least two independent clauses and at least one subordinate clause.

■ Exercise 1.9

In the blank following each sentence, indicate whether the sentence is simple, compound, complex, or compound-complex. Check your answers on page 122. If you make a mistake, review section **1f** of the *Handbook*.

1. A car compass is easy to install and simple to adjust.

   ____

2. Although our new gas lawn mower is more powerful, our old electric mower is more reliable.

   ____

3. Finally arriving on June 21, his birthday present was almost a month late.

   ____

4. Mr. Martinez and I disagree about how much foreign investment is healthy, but we do agree on free trade.

   ____

5. When her psychoanalyst decided to sail around the world in a small boat, Sonia felt abandoned, as if she had been cut adrift.

   ____

6. Stanley's parents resented his borrowing the truck without their permission, so on his birthday, they gave him a bus pass.

   ____

7. The secretary insisted on knowing who was calling before he would accept the charges.

   ____

8. According to most scholars, she is the author of the sonnets.

   ____

9. If it hadn't been for your antique car, we would have been home by now, and I would be relaxing in a bathtub full of hot, soapy water.

   ____

10. He was the last one over the finish line, but he made it just the same.

    ____

2 Sentence Fragments

A **fragment** is a group of words that begins with a capital letter and ends with a period but forms only part of a sentence. As a rule, do not write sentence fragments.

2a

Phrases are sometimes mistakenly punctuated as sentences.

2b

Subordinate clauses are sometimes mistakenly punctuated as sentences.

■ Exercise 2.1

Some of the following groups of words consist of correct sentences, and some include fragments. Indicate whether each group contains a fragment error or is correct. Check your answers on page 122. If you make more than one mistake, review **Chapter 2** of the *Handbook* before going on.

1. With snow a metre deep in places and the snowplow not likely to go through for another hour.

   ____

2. Maria, opening the curtains to look out and seeing that it was going to be a beautiful, sunny day.

   ____

3. Tennis, she knew, would never earn her a living. But she loved the game nonetheless.

   ____

4. The provincial champions had gathered for the national spelling bee. Dictionaries stamped on their brains and their heads teeming with stumpers.

   ____

5. Why would anyone name a cat "Squirrel"? Nuts!

   ____

6. Ahmad, investing in a new pair of shoes and a new suit, even though he could not afford it, wanting to look his best for the interview.

   ____

7. Watching one football game after another, with New Year's Day just slipping by and no one even thinking about making resolutions.

   ____

8. Standing in the trees and trying to light his pipe in spite of the brisk wind, Holmes suddenly saw, to his amazement, a huge hound bearing down on him.

   ____

9. Trog the Troll had dreamed for many years of joining the Superheroes' Club. During the long, damp nights underneath his ancestral bridge.

   ____

10. The old judge, still thinking faster than most of the young lawyers, which means they prepare carefully for appearances in his courtroom.

    ____

■ Exercise 2.2

Some of the following groups of words consist of correct sentences, and some include fragments. Indicate whether each group contains a fragment error or is correct. Check your answers on page 123. If you make more than one mistake, review **Chapter 2** of the *Handbook* before going on.

1. As complicated as it may at first seem, a rose, given a wide range of alternative names, smelling sweetly still.

   ____

2. Although nobody could prove it, all felt that the ad campaign was a hoax.

   ____

3. Standing in the rain beside the chicken coop, the newly painted red wheelbarrow, shedding water in large beads.

   ____

4. Not being able to keep from laughing in serious situations, a good way to offend people unintentionally.

   ____

5. Plant diseases, which are often caused by fungi, bacteria, and viruses, just as many diseases that afflict human beings are.

   ____

6. Finally, after what seemed like many hours in the waiting room. Another false alarm!

   ____

7. Could it possibly have been the mice that ate my lunch?

   ____

8. Fatima studied very hard. And, when the grades were announced, learned that she would graduate with first-class honours.

   ____

9. "No cause for alarm!" announced the flight attendant, refolding the oxygen mask back into the storage panel.

   ____

10. Sentence fragments are comparatively rare in formal expository writing. Notwithstanding their suitability for some purposes.

   ____

■ Exercise 2.3

Some of the following groups of words consist of correct sentences, and some include fragments. Indicate whether each group contains a fragment error or is correct. Check your answers on page 123. If you make more than one mistake, review **Chapter 2** of the *Handbook* before going on.

1. Spending many hours in the library, because of procrastination earlier on, in order to finish the report by the deadline.

   ____

2. The Californian who designed our office building knew little of our Canadian winters and deserves to work here in January.

   ____

3. The legal aid office, which offers legal advice and representation to people who can't afford a lawyer.

   ____

4. The road to Cambridge Narrows is impassable to all but four-wheel-drive vehicles. Especially when it rains.

   ____

5. Crusoe would have preferred to stay at home and live a quiet, middle-class life. That is, of course, just what his father had advised him to do.

   ____

6. A large field enclosed by tiered seats, otherwise known as a stadium, and the home of rock concerts and football games.

____

7. The alpine coughs, which are a type of crow living on Himalayan peaks as well as in the Alps, fly well at high altitude.

____

8. Just because you haven't seen any car accidents for a few weeks. Can you afford to stop driving defensively?

____

9. Pilar, having been asked by the producer to design the costumes for *Blood Relations*, has consented.

____

10. Most of the members of the council left the meeting early today. Which is, of course, what usually happens.

____

3 Comma Splices and Fused Sentences

Do not link two main clauses with only a comma (comma splice) or run two main clauses together without any punctuation (fused sentence).

3a
Commas occur between independent clauses only when they are linked by a co-ordinating conjunction (*and, but, or, for, nor, so, yet.*) (See also 18a.)

3b
Semicolons occur before conjunctive adverbs or transitional phrases that are placed between independent clauses. (See also 18a.)

3c
Divided quotations can trick you into making a comma splice. (See also Chapter 20.)

■ Exercise 3.1

Some of the following groups of words are correct sentences, and some contain comma splice and fused sentence errors. If a sentence is incorrect, indicate the nature of the error—comma splice or fused sentence—in the blank that follows, and underline the point at which the incorrect link occurs. If a sentence contains no error, write "correct" in the blank. Check your answers on page 123. If you make more than one error, review **Chapter 3** in the *Handbook* before going on to the next exercise.

1. By noon, the snow was over a metre deep in drifts and falling steadily, the snowplows would not reach the side roads till the storm was over.

   ____

2. When Marina realized it was beginning to rain, she ran to get her umbrella, it was not hanging in the closet where she had left it.

   ____

3. "I finally went to see the movie *The House on Haunted Hill*," Nicole admitted "I had been warned where to expect the scary parts and knew when to shut my eyes."

   ____

4. The river kept on rising it was almost up to the boardwalk; then the flood seemed to reach its crest.

____

5. A birch bark or hollowed bone horn is often used to call in moose although many of the old-timers will simply blow through tightly gripped hands.

____

6. "A sea otter is an excellent swimmer," explained the tour guide, "Can any of you swim on your back while smashing clams on a rock balanced on your stomach?"

____

7. Because the storm struck in the night, the snowplows were able to clear the parkway traffic moved slowly but steadily in the morning.

____

8. Antoine could barely afford a haircut, yet he wanted to look his best for the job interview.

____

9. Nikos wanted to be a great novelist, however, he changed his mind after taking a correspondence course in creative writing.

____

10. Mrs. Novak admitted that the population explosion was a serious problem, on the other hand, she loved babies.

____

■ Exercise 3.2

Some of the following groups of words are correct sentences, and some contain comma splice and fused sentence errors. If a sentence is incorrect, indicate the nature of the error—comma splice or fused sentence—in the blank that follows, and underline the point at which the incorrect link occurs. If a sentence contains no error, write "correct" in the blank. Check your answers on page 123. If you make more than one error, review **Chapter 3** in the *Handbook* before going on to the next exercise.

1. I cleared the table and washed the dishes then I swept the floor.

____

2. Some finicky cats are so spoiled they won't even eat real meat, mine absolutely refuses to eat liver, it doesn't matter if it's cooked or not.

____

3. The telephone woke me up at 3:00 A.M., it was a wrong number.

____

4. The car wouldn't move another centimetre, we had run out of gas.

____

5. The dog was bored, he was whining and getting on everyone's nerves.

____

6. "Would you look at Fang wag his tail!" exclaimed Juan, "he just loves those beef biscuits."

____

7. The ice was as smooth as glass it was just perfect for skating.

____

8. I set the oven for 190°C, then I prepared the batter for the cake.

____

9. We skied from morning till dark and then, after thawing out enough to feel the floor under our feet, we danced and played shuffleboard until midnight.

____

10. Camping in the Rockies, we saw elk, mountain goats, and many different kinds of birds, however, the Canada jays stole most of our lunch.

____

■ Exercise 3.3

Some of the following groups of words are correct sentences, and some contain comma splice and fused sentence errors. If a sentence is incorrect, indicate the nature of the error—comma splice or fused sentence—in the blank that follows, and underline the point at which the incorrect link occurs. If a sentence contains no error, write "correct" in the blank. Check your answers on pages 123–24. If you make more than one error, review **Chapter 3** in the *Handbook* before going on to the next exercise.

1. It was nearly two o'clock, still the mail hadn't arrived, it was usually here in the morning.

____

2. Jogging is a great sport, it requires only a pair of sneakers, can be done anywhere by anyone, and is an excellent form of exercise.

____

3. Pressing her bag against her side and holding on to her hat, the young woman ran frantically after the bus that was pulling away from the curb.

____

4. We can take the scenic route through the mountains; we can leave early it won't matter if we're a few minutes late.

____

5. Having lost the patient, the tree surgeon spent a quiet moment contemplating the debris.

____

6. I wouldn't tease the sharks along the Great Barrier Reef if I were you, after all, who wants to die without ever having seen a live wallaby?

____

7. Nina is reading *The Lord of the Rings* again she says the symbolism is intriguing.

____

8. She cut through the stranger's backyard, not knowing that a pitbull was tied there, being very quiet, waiting for her to come within reach of its chain.

____

9. The coffee was so strong that it coated his teeth and tongue and throat, it was made just the way he liked it.

____

10. "You decide what to bring me, Santa, I want it to be a surprise."

____

■ Exercise 3.4

Some of the following groups of words are correct sentences, and some contain comma splice and fused sentence errors. If a sentence is incorrect, indicate the nature of the error—comma splice or fused sentence—in the blank that follows and underline the point at which the incorrect link occurs. If a sentence contains no error, write "correct" in the blank. Check your answers on page 124. If you make more than one error, review **Chapter 3** in the *Handbook* before going on to the next exercise.

1. It rained the entire month of May still, by late July, there was talk of crop failure because of drought.

____

2. "Boudreau, by far the most experienced member of the team," reported the announcer, "is far ahead of the other cyclists."

____

3. We mowed the lawn, trimmed the hedge, and swept the walks, the yard looked beautiful!

____

4. Taking our pig to the veterinarian is always so embarrassing, why can't we have a dog or cat like other families?

____

5. Albert raced up the front steps, flung open the door, threw his books in the corner then he turned his full attention to his favourite refrigerator.

____

6. Some farmers raise bees, not only for the honey, which they can sell, but also because bees help pollinate many kinds of crops.

____

7. The little kittens tumbled in the long grass, warmed by the sun, they were content to let their mother rest.

____

8. When my wallet was stolen, I was left penniless in a foreign country, I couldn't even pay my hotel bill.

____

9. Lady's puppies yipped and yapped all night never did they give her a moment of peace.

____

10. "Don't think your worries are over when the plane touches down," Amelia warned, "getting out of the airport quickly is the real challenge."

____

4 Adjectives and Adverbs

Adjectives and adverbs are modifiers that qualify, restrict, or intensify the meaning of other words. They also describe degrees of comparison. It is important to understand the distinction between adjectives and adverbs and to use the appropriate forms of each.

4a

Adverbs modify verbs, adjectives, and other adverbs.

4b

There is a distinction between adverbs used to modify verbs and adjectives used as subject or object complements.

■ Exercise 4.1

In each of the following sentences, underline the correct modifier in parentheses. Check your answers on page 124. If you make more than one error, review sections **4**, **4a**, and **4b** in the *Handbook* before going on to the next exercise.

1. "All aboard," said the captain very (loudly, loud).
2. The brown fox jumps (quick, quickly) over the lazy dog.
3. The street person looked (hungry, hungrily) as he prepared to taste the stew.
4. The hobo tasted the stew (hungry, hungrily).
5. They observed antelope running at speeds of (near, nearly) sixty kilometres an hour.
6. If those antelope were big enough to pull sulkies, they (sure, surely) would have looked (good, well) at the racetrack.
7. Anna came (awful, awfully) close to saying things she would have regretted later, but she held her tongue.
8. (Merry, Merrily) sang the Christmas choir.
9. Marie looked (graceful, gracefully) skating across the rink.
10. Speaking (clear, clearly) gives added force to whatever you have to say.

■ Exercise 4.2

Correct any adjectives or adverbs misused in the following sentences by placing the incorrect word or words in square brackets and writing the correct form in the blank following each sentence. Some sentences may contain more than one mistake, and some may be correct. Check your answers on page 124. If you make more than one error, review sections **4**, **4a**, and **4b** in the *Handbook*, and make sure you understand your mistakes before going on to the next exercise.

1. Often the tidal wave that follows an earthquake is more terrible devastating than the earthquake itself.

   ____

2. Rosemary was elated that her guests found the meal so well.

   ____

3. The study was especially persuasive because its sources were documented so accurate and thoroughly.

   ____

4. Jacques felt really badly about the damage his pet had done in the van.

   ____

5. Slow but sure, Mr. Chan struggled through night course after night course in pursuit of his accounting degree.

   ____

6. The sun shines brightly in my old Kentucky home.

   ____

7. As careful as his pack and heavy boots would allow, Dietrich traversed the avalanche slope.

   ____

8. Tanned and relaxed after her business trip to Brazil, Gina looked so healthily that the marketing manager was surprised to learn that all had gone good.

   ____

9. Near all my weekends until the end of March will be taken up with writing term papers.

   ____

10. Surely you don't intend to cross Lake Superior in a canoe!

   ____

4c

Many adjectives and adverbs change form to indicate the degree of comparison.

Use the appropriate forms of adjectives and adverbs for the comparative and the superlative:

(1) The comparative denotes a greater degree or refers to two in a comparison.

(2) The superlative denotes the greatest degree or refers to three or more in a comparison.

(3) A double comparative or superlative is incorrect.

■ Exercise 4.3

In each of the following sentences, underline the correct comparative or superlative form of the modifiers in parentheses. Check your answers on page 125. If you make more than one error, review **4c** of the *Handbook* and make sure you understand your mistakes before going on to the next exercise.

1. Lynn is the (friendlier, friendliest) of the twins.
2. Dr. Gatz was the (most skilful, skilfulest) brain surgeon in the country.
3. Of all animals on earth, the cheetah can run the (most fast, fastest).
4. Joyce's later fiction is (more hard, harder, more harder) to read than the stories in *Dubliners*.
5. Schliemann was the (most unique, more unique, most nearly unique) person Jurgis had ever met.
6. Georgia had the (worst, worse, worstest, most bad) struggle in her life as she tried to persuade people to sign her petition.
7. The sun seems (brilliantest, most brilliant) on crisp, clear days in late winter.
8. Roxanne is the (best, better) among the bridge players in the club.
9. The (costliest, most costly) car is not always the most reliable.
10. Of the two answers, the one (most correct, more nearly correct, most nearly correct) is underlined.

■ Exercise 4.4

Correct any errors in the comparative or superlative forms of modifiers in the following sentences by placing the incorrect word or words in square brackets and writing the correct form in the blank following each sentence. Some sentences may contain more than one mistake, and some may be correct. Check your answers on page 125. If you make more than one error, review **4c** of the *Handbook* carefully and make sure you understand your mistakes before trying the next exercise.

1. Cinderella wore her very best dress to the ball.

   ____

2. Ahmed ran as quick as he could, but others in the race ran faster.

   ____

3. We consider the North Face the best of the two standard routes on the mountain.

   ____

4. Sheldon, whose mother was an orthodontist, had the most perfect teeth.

   ____

5. The older of his four sons stayed home to help run the family farm.

   ____

6. The play was the most funniest in the festival.

   ____

7. September was more warm than July last year.

   ____

8. It was the best of times and the worst of times.

   ____

9. Jupiter was the jovialest of the Roman gods.

   ____

10. My flu was worst at New Year's than it was at Christmas.

   ____

4d
Use of a word group or a noun as an adjective can be awkward or ambiguous.

4e
A single rather than a double negative is correct.

■ Exercise 4.5

Correct any errors in the forms of modifiers in the following sentences. Place any modifier used incorrectly in square brackets, and write the correct form in the blank. Some sentences may contain more than one mistake, and some may be correct. Check your answers on page 125. If you make no mistakes, skip the last exercise and move on to the next chapter; otherwise, review **Chapter 4** of the *Handbook* before going on to the next exercise.

1. Driving reckless almost cost Kail his life.

   ____

2. It was difficult to judge which was the better of the three pies.

____

3. Walk soft and carry a big stick.

____

4. Monique and Michel enjoyed the food muchly during their trip to the East Coast.

____

5. The oranges in Lorenzo's groves were the most nearly perfect to be found.

____

6. The children were behaving bad because they had decided to test the baby-sitter's limits.

____

7. Carlos held onto the rope tight, scared of falling or being knocked off the steep slope by falling ice, rocks, or goats.

____

8. Her editor felt surely that her novel could be completed in time.

____

9. Before he joined the gun club, Freeman hadn't never given any thought to the dangers of firearms.

____

10. Ketchup tastes well on hot dogs, hamburgers, French fries, and even on scrambled eggs.

____

■ Exercise 4.6

Correct any errors in the forms of modifiers in the following sentences. Place any modifier used incorrectly in square brackets, and write the correct form in the blank. Some sentences may contain more than one mistake, and some may be correct. Check your answers on page 125–26. If you make no mistakes, you should be able to handle the forms of adjectives and adverbs confidently. If you do make any mistakes, reread **Chapter 4** of the *Handbook* carefully.

1. If you are real careful, you can remove a sliver almost painless.

____

2. She felt near dead from exhaustion after swimming across Lake Ontario.

____

3. Granny Schultz looked on affectionate at the children as they redecorated her living room.

____

4. Randy sure had a reputation to live up to.

____

5. Which one of those two pumpkins is more nearly round?

____

6. Although he grew up in a tiny, backward community, his fame is now internationally.

____

7. Dimitri felt that he had always been treated unfair by his older brothers and sisters.

____

8. Professor Narayan considered the find most exceptional.

____

9. After her vacation, Elsa's complexion was the darker of any in the office.

____

10. The audience clapped whole-hearted as the opera concluded.

____

5 Coherence: Misplaced Parts and Dangling Modifiers

5a

Placing modifiers near the words they modify clarifies meaning.

(1) In formal English, place modifiers such as *almost, only, just, even, hardly, nearly,* and *merely* immediately before the words they modify for emphasis and clarification of meaning.

(2) Place a modifying prepositional phrase to indicate clearly what the phrase modifies.

(3) Place adjective clauses near the words they modify.

(4) Revise "squinting" constructions—modifiers that may refer to either a preceding or a following word.

(5) Revise awkward constructions that split an infinitive.

■ Exercise 5.1

Revise the following sentences to correct undesirable separation of related parts. Some sentences may be correct. Check your answers on page 126. If you make one mistake, be sure you understand your error before going on to the next exercise. If you make more than one mistake, review section **5a** of the *Handbook*.

1. The old gentleman who was walking slowly caught up with the young couple.
2. Most of us like to speak well of those who have departed from this world in spite of their faults.
3. The life of Hagar Shipley is the subject of Margaret Laurence's *The Stone Angel,* which lasts well into old age.
4. Although Boris delivers papers in the mornings, he almost makes it to school on time every day.
5. The goalie had not even found his pads by the time the game was supposed to start.
6. Fancy Dancer was thoroughly rubbed down by the groom who had just galloped round the track in record time.
7. Before long, they were able to fundamentally and permanently change the procedures for hiring casual staff.
8. Davy Crockett is supposed to have killed a bear at the tender age of three.

9. In no uncertain terms, the desk clerk informed us that no pets were allowed in the hotel suites.
10. Mrs. Bates sat in a chair in her bedroom which rocked incessantly.

■ Exercise 5.2

Revise the following sentences to correct undesirable separation of related parts. Some sentences may be correct. Check your answers on page 126–27. If you make one mistake, be sure you understand your error before going on to the next exercise. If you make more than one mistake, review section **5a** of the *Handbook*.

1. Everyone present knew that to immediately get the injured child to a hospital was essential.
2. My sister says she wants only to hike along the Bruce Trail on her trip to Ontario this summer.
3. We purchased a grand piano from an elderly gentleman weighing at least four hundred kilograms.
4. Bonny's husband announced that she had just given birth to twins by telephone.
5. The buffalo bounded after my girlfriend, huge, hairy, and primitive looking.
6. Pierre bought new outfits for his dancers that went for $49.95 on special.
7. His jeans were covered with grass stains that were faded blue.
8. The children found a nest built by birds made of straw, mud, and string.
9. These new laws allow anyone to get a divorce whose marriage has broken down in less than three months.
10. Eating spicy foods quickly irritates an ulcer.

5b

There are several ways to revise dangling modifiers.

A dangling modifier is a word or, more often, a phrase that does not clearly refer to another word or word group in a sentence.

■ Exercise 5.3

Revise the following sentences to eliminate dangling modifiers. Some sentences may be correct. Check your answers on page 127. Your revisions may vary somewhat from the samples provided without being incorrect. If you make a mistake, review section **5b** of the *Handbook* before going on to the next exercise.

1. After feeding the dog, putting the cat out, and getting the coffee machine ready for the morning, it was nearly two hours before I could get to sleep.
2. Drinking four cups of coffee just to wake up, the day was going to be a long one for certain.
3. Lurking behind the theatre, his Honda's stereo was stolen by thieves.
4. Snapping at the air and slobbering freely, the warden shot the rabid wolf.
5. After finishing an assignment and eating a quick lunch, the bell rang indicating that it was time for the afternoon classes to begin.
6. Unable to stand the strain of his job, the psychologist was Ali's last resort.
7. While still in the fourth grade, Robin's parents attempted to explain the facts of life to her.
8. When competently directed, I find live theatre most entertaining.
9. Facing up to the realities of cancer presented a challenge greater than any Hon-Wah had had to face before.
10. Finally, after what seemed like many hours in the waiting room, the doctor announced that it was yet another false alarm.

■ Exercise 5.4

Revise the following sentences to eliminate dangling modifiers. Some sentences may be correct. Check your answers on page 127 Your revisions may vary somewhat from the samples provided without being incorrect. If you make a mistake, review section **5b** of the *Handbook* carefully.

1. To become a professional athlete, a great deal of practice is required.
2. To succeed in any endeavour, commitment is necessary.
3. Humming a lively tune, Mr. Bee went in search of some delicious nectar.
4. When thinking of investing in real estate, titles must be searched before buying.
5. While rowing home, a storm came up suddenly.
6. Guided by the directions on the box, the doll's house is supposed to assemble very quickly.
7. Under the circumstances, it is hardly surprising that Antonio won.
8. After eating even snacks, your teeth should be brushed thoroughly.

9. Pedalling his mountain bike at top speed, the bear pursued poor Herman.
10. Without showing any emotion whatsoever, the sentence of execution by firing squad was handed down by the judge.

6 Pronouns

6a
Pronouns agree with their antecedents.

■ Exercise 6.1
In each of the following sentences, find the antecedent of the pronouns in parentheses, and then underline the correct pronoun. Check your answers on pages 127–28. If you have more than one error, review sections **6** and **6a** of the *Handbook* before going on to the next exercise.

1. One is capable of overcoming seemingly impossible obstacles in life if (her, their) attitude is positive enough.
2. The committee was aware of the controversial nature of the proposal and chose (its, their) spokesperson with care.
3. Neither Prospero nor the other revellers were able to resist (his, their) uninvited guest.
4. The team understands its main weakness and will concentrate on offence on (their, its) next road trip.
5. Every player has (their, his) specific responsibilities for preventing shots on goal.
6. The board is aware that (its, their) inquiries are accomplishing nothing.
7. Everyone was able to make it to shore, even though (they, he) had to fight (their, his) way through high surf to do it.
8. Everybody was studying hard for (their, his) final examinations.
9. If the ratings do not soon improve, neither Bubbles the Clown nor his animal buddies will have (his, their) cozy home on Happy Street much longer.
10. The members of the jury are refusing to reveal (its, their) verdict until lunch has been served.

■ Exercise 6.2
Correct the errors in agreement in the following sentences. Avoid making unnecessary changes. Check your answers on page 128. If you make any errors, be sure you understand why before going on to the next exercise. Review **Chapter 6** of the *Handbook* if you are in doubt.

1. The public address system asked whether anyone had lost their tickets.
2. At the first sight of its idols, the audience surged forward as if they were a living creature.

3. All those competing must be in top physical condition to assure himself of having a genuine chance.
4. Nobody wants the deficit to grow, but nobody wants to see their taxes raised either.
5. Each swimmer in the pool should know where their buddy is at all times.
6. No one knows how many hours go into restoring antique furniture until they do it themselves.
7. The committee members stood up and applauded to welcome its new chairperson.
8. Each of the three novelists may be said to have developed a voice all their own.
9. The news media did its part in exposing the problem of political patronage.
10. If the review board decides to roll back wages, our union will appeal their decision.

6b
Pronouns usually refer to the nouns immediately preceding them.

A pronoun should refer unmistakably to its antecedent. The further away a pronoun is from its antecedent, the more likely it is that confusion will occur. Pronouns such as *it*, *this*, *that*, *which*, and *such* may refer to the sense of a clause, sentence, or paragraph, as well as to a specific word or phrase, but broad or implied references can be unclear and should be made explicit.

■ Exercise 6.3
Revise the following sentences to eliminate awkward or confusing pronoun references. Check your answers on pages 128–29. If you make a mistake, review section **6b** of the *Handbook* before trying the next exercise.

1. That zebra would look a lot like our pony if it were not for its colour.
2. Arbour Day is observed in some provinces by planting trees; this seems harmless.
3. The twins gave interesting reports in class this morning, but they sounded a lot alike.
4. Only after her mother had been dead for over a year did Corina learn that she had been adopted.
5. Li-Ying remembered leaving her parka in a trunk, but she couldn't find it.

6. The dog was left chained in the yard by his master who was trained to attack intruders.
7. A park with many shade trees is located in the ravine behind our backyard, which is always cool even in the middle of summer.
8. While Marika was helping her mother wash the car, she accidentally sprayed her with the hose.
9. On the map it shows the Hudson's Bay Building as being just west of City Hall.
10. Taking no warm clothing in their packs and only enough food for lunch, they took the fork to the left, which turned out to be a serious mistake.

■ Exercise 6.4

Revise the following sentences to eliminate awkward or confusing pronoun references. Check your answers on page 129. If you make a mistake, review section **6b** of the *Handbook* before trying the next exercise.

1. Inga carefully explained to Amelia that she had put up with far more from her fiancé than any woman ought to.
2. The windows on the taxis are dirty, so they really ought to be washed.
3. The Simons continued to quarrel with the Wongs over their dog's barking and the complaints to the police.
4. Marvin moved away from home last spring; his mother was completely unable to cope with it.
5. My mother informs me that parents never stop worrying about their children—no matter how old they become.
6. The instruction booklet that comes with the camera is carefully worded, so purchasers should have no trouble understanding how to use it.
7. Eric finally decided to go to the veterinarian with the puppy who had advised him about horse liniment.
8. Leonard's father, an automobile mechanic, found time to teach him how to do basic repairs when he was thirty.
9. Even though he finds a brook trout's bones a nuisance to remove, Serge eats them whenever he can get them.
10. Waiters have to work nights, of course, but the tips are good, and Rodrigo doesn't seem to mind it.

■ Exercise 6.5

Revise the following sentences to eliminate awkward or confusing pronoun references. Some sentences may be correct. Check your answers on pages 129–30. If you make a mistake, review section **6b** of the *Handbook* carefully.

1. To enjoy your vacation, you sometimes must work at relaxing.
2. Depressed prices make it a good time to invest in real estate, and it is an attractive property.
3. Amelia and Claudia find going to college in Quebec challenging because they speak a different language there.
4. After watching the program about fleas on pets, Marco remarked to Mikos that he thought he ought to have Shaggy treated.
5. Because Martine and her mother are the same size, she often borrows her clothing.
6. Otto met Leo in the park when he was on his lunch break.
7. The old bear returned to the beaver lodge day after day, but they always managed to elude him.
8. He followed the path on his bicycle in the evening gloom, which was made tricky by numerous baseball-size rocks.
9. In the handout sheets introducing the course, it made the dangers of plagiarism very clear.
10. The retired marshal was surprised to find himself approached by the townspeople who had hung up his guns forever.

6c
Pronoun form in compound constructions varies.

6d
The use of a pronoun in its own clause determines its case.

■ Exercise 6.6
In each of the following sentences, underline the correct form of the pronouns in parentheses. Check your answers on page 130 If you make one error, be sure you understand why before going on to the next exercise. If you make more than one error, review sections **6c** and **6d** before going on.

1. The receptionist wanted to know (who, whom) I was calling.
2. This birthday gift was sent by (who, whom)?
3. Between you and (I, me), not one of the supervisors has any formal training.
4. The deed to the property is registered in the names of my brother and (I, me).
5. With (who, whom) have you been spending your time lately?

6. You will never be able to guess (who, whom) the new owner of the house on the corner is.
7. The old dirt bike would rarely run more than a few minutes for my brother or (me, I).
8. To (whom, who) do you think the Oscar for best actress will be going this year?
9. Her most valued possession is an autographed copy of *Anne of Green Gables* by Lucy Maud Montgomery, (whom, who) she admires a great deal.
10. (Who, Whom) are the Tremblays taking along on their trip to Florida?

■ Exercise 6.7

In each of the following sentences, underline the correct form of the pronouns in parentheses. Check your answers on page 130. If you make a mistake, review sections **6c** and **6d** carefully before going on.

1. The premier and (me, I) disagree on the issue of how much foreign investment is healthy.
2. Very soon we will have to meet with (whoever, whomever) the union has placed on the committee.
3. Send the shipment to (whoever, whomever) is next on the waiting list.
4. (Who, Whom) is Jeannie rooming with in residence?
5. The security guard explained to Jessica and (I, me) that the auditorium would not be open for another two hours.
6. The point is not (who, whom) found the wallet, but (who, whom) the rightful owner is.
7. I would really like to know (who, whom) we will find to chair the selection committee.
8. (Who, Whom) did you see at the concert?
9. Chandra and (her, she) will be designing the costumes for the production of *The Ecstasy of Rita Joe*.
10. (Who, Whom) is responsible for seeing that the commercials are aired at the proper times?

6e

A pronoun before a gerund uses the possessive form.

6f

Pronouns use the objective form for the subject or the object of an infinitive.

6g
Pronouns use the subjective form for a subject complement.

■ Exercise 6.8
In each of the following sentences, underline the correct form of the pronouns in parentheses. Check your answers on page 130. If you make one error, be sure you understand why before going on to the next exercise. If you make more than one error, review sections **6e**, **6f**, and **6g** of the *Handbook* before going on.

1. His mother did not like (him, his) borrowing the car without permission.
2. The last one over the finish line was (he, him).
3. Do you think that it could possibly have been (him, he) who ate Mr. Duvalier's lunch?
4. If the person making the decisions were (me, I), I would never raise tuition.
5. With (I, me, my) being elected as class president, I was assured at least one afternoon off a month to attend a council meeting.
6. It's up to (you and me, you and I) to repair the doorstep.
7. What got me in trouble was (my, me) not being able to keep from laughing even during the most serious situations.
8. If it hadn't been for (you, your) sleeping in, we would have arrived by now.
9. Monique was not grateful that Manuel wanted (she, her) to make a career of inspiring his poetry.
10. If it is to (me, my) skipping classes that you are referring, please just say so.

■ Exercise 6.9
In each of the following sentences, underline the correct form of the pronouns in parentheses. Check your answers on page 130. Referring to sections **6** and **6a–6g** in the *Handbook*, if necessary, make sure you understand your errors before going on to the next chapter.

1. Just between (you and I, you and me), I think the play was a disaster.
2. The teacher gave (Jacob and I, Jacob and me) a lecture about getting to class on time.
3. The counsellors always make sure they know (whom, who) to call in case of an emergency.

4. I intend to support the athlete (who, whom) the newspapers say is crossing the country in a wheelchair.
5. Remember the importance of (they, them, their) adapting to the high altitude before attempting the summit.
6. (She and I, She and me, Her and I, Her and me) left early.
7. Give (him and me, he and me, he and I, him and I) all your money or you're not going to be invited to another robbery.
8. The architect (who, whom) I think designed our office building was from California and knew little of Canadian winters.
9. Instead of (he, him) and his friend from Calgary, we are inviting representatives from Saskatchewan.
10. Soon after the polls closed, the newscasters announced (who, whom) the winner was likely to be.

7 Verbs

Verbs express the action in a sentence. They show what someone (or something) does, whether the subject is singular or plural, what its relationship to the audience (first, second, or third person) is, when an action occurred, who did it, and whether it is hypothetical or conditional. They are the heart of the sentence.

7a
Verbs must agree with their subjects.

■ Exercise 7.1
In each of the following sentences, underline the correct verb in parentheses. Check your answers on page 130. If you make one error, be sure you understand your mistake before going on to the next exercise. If you make more than one error, review sections **7** and **7a** of the *Handbook.*

1. There, beside the barn, (is, are) the hen and her chickens.
2. Our summer cottage, along with three hectares of land, (is, are) for sale.
3. Neither the building blocks nor the teddy bear (is, are) of any interest to this television-obsessed child.
4. Kassem is one of those handymen who always (finds, find) interesting projects to keep him busy.
5. This is rapidly becoming one of those situations that (calls, call) for drastic action.
6. This self-styled Robin Hood, together with several assistant outlaws, (live, lives) in a nearby forest and (make, makes) plans for redistributing wealth.
7. There (is, are) three reasons why I don't approve of smoking—at least.
8. Here (is, are) your coat and boats.
9. Each boy and each girl in the rhythm band (play, plays) at least two instruments.
10. One of the few things that little Maria will eat consistently (are, is) carrots.

■ Exercise 7.2
In each of the following sentences, underline the correct verb in parentheses. Check your answers on page 131. If you make any errors, review sections **7** and **7a** of the *Handbook* before going on.

1. One of the running backs on the opposing team (was, were) injured during the game.
2. Hudson's *Green Mansions* (is, are) definitely romantic fiction.
3. Scabies (come, comes) from mites laying eggs under the skin.
4. Throughout the summer, a gaggle of geese (live, lives) in their yard.
5. Mr. Chung's investment in the project (were, was) three years of his life.
6. Either of them (is, are) capable of succeeding in university.
7. Twelve dollars (seem, seems) like a lot to pay for a short cab ride.
8. What he liked most about the new breakfast cereal (were, was) the trading cards included in the packages.
9. Mathematics (help, helps) one to study economics.
10. We nearly missed the ferry because a flock of sheep (was, were) crossing the road in front of the car.

■ Exercise 7.3

Correct the errors in agreement between subjects and verbs in the following sentences. Some sentences may be correct. Check your answers on page 131. If you make one error, be sure you understand your mistake before going on to the next exercise. If you make more than one error, review sections **7** and **7a** of the *Handbook* carefully.

1. The doctor on duty, not to mention the nurses who were also working in emergency that night, say that it was the worst accident in years.
2. One of the most common complaints of climbers at high altitude are headaches.
3. They, not I, am going to watch the Grey Cup parade this afternoon.
4. Neither prefers to go first.
5. *The Diviners* by Margaret Laurence are very moving.
6. Being able to afford a swimming pool is one of the things that makes work worthwhile.
7. The cat, as well as four new kittens, were on the doorstep in the morning.
8. Each of his other daughters has made the same decision before.
9. Over my door sits that wretched raven and his buddy the crow.
10. Neither Mama Bear nor Papa Bear like the idea of little blond girls paying uninvited calls.

7b
Verbs have at least three principal parts.

7c
Tense forms express differences in time.

■ Exercise 7.4
Underline the correct verb form in parentheses in the following sentences. Check your answers on page 131. If you make one mistake, be sure you understand why before trying the next exercise. If you make more than one mistake, review sections **7b** and **7c** of the *Handbook*.

1. If you had not (sat, set) around all summer on the beach, you would not have to work part time this semester.
2. Mr. Valente stopped worrying about his chickens because he (has seen, saw) no tracks around the coop for over a month.
3. The community picnic was postponed because the river (has flooded, flooded) the park.
4. As usual, some of the fans will have run out onto the field before the final gun (sounded, has sounded).
5. Now I (lie, lay) me down to sleep.
6. After we had spent six dismal days in cramped tents waiting for the snow to stop, the guide (demanded, has demanded) his fee.
7. Having finally completed high school, Seeta (felt, has felt) she was ready to take on the world.
8. In my opinion, Benny was lying when he said he had (laid, lain) under a tree the whole night.
9. It is standard practice (to post, to have posted) teaching evaluations on the Web.
10. When the new combined program in science and education is available, it (will give, will have given) students plenty of time to choose specializations.

■ Exercise 7.5
Some of the following sentences contain errors in verb forms, and some are correct. Correct the mistakes, and write "correct" after the sentences that contain no errors. Check your answers on pages 131–32. They need not be exactly the same as those supplied, but they should be similar. If you make one mistake, be sure you understand why before going on to the next exercise. If you make more than one mistake, review sections **7b** and **7c** of the *Handbook*.

1. Serving his time, Mugsie left prison a reformed man.
2. Scheele discovered oxygen in 1772, but it has been there all along.
3. The Ruskins had payed for their trip in advance, so they were afraid of losing their vacation when the cruise line went bankrupt.
4. Come in and set down!
5. As the weeks passed, it became clear to Malcolm that some of the men in the logging camp were prejudice against university students.
6. Mrs. Singh has been driving for over forty years when she fell asleep at the wheel and came to rest amid the sympathy cards at her local pharmacy.
7. You will need to hurry to catch them now because they were gone for nearly half an hour.
8. If you had ran all the way over here, you would not be late now.
9. Although he was in good shape generally, Ali found that he was not use to all the bending and lifting he was required to do.
10. Because the spring rain has finally began to fall, the grass is beginning to turn green.

7d
Although rare, the subjunctive mood is still used for specific purposes.

7e
Unnecessary shifts in tense or mood can confuse readers. (See also 8e.)

■ Exercise 7.6
Underline the correct verb form in parentheses in the following sentences. Check your answers on page 132. If you make one mistake, be sure you understand why before going on to the next exercise. If you make more than one mistake, review sections **7c** and **7d** of the *Handbook.*

1. If the weather (would have been, had been) bearable, there would have been a better turnout at the rally.
2. First Natalia watered the lawn; then she (plays, played) softball.
3. If you expect to be out in the rain, and you will work hard while there, you (need, will need) rainwear that allows perspiration to escape.
4. If I (was, were) you, I would concentrate on improving the way I use verbs.
5. Our neighbours (had, have) three dogs that bark and bark.

6. It is required that he (makes, make) up all the work he missed even though he was sick.
7. Dr. Renaud finally recommended that Mr. Weslosky (sees, see) a specialist.
8. I wish I (would have been, had been) born rich so I would not have had to work for a living.
9. Rather than just throwing old clothing away, you (should, would) remember those less fortunate than you.
10. Off they (go, went), and they were singing at the top of their lungs going over the hill.

■ Exercise 7.7

Some of the following sentences contain errors in verb forms, and some are correct. Correct the mistakes, and write "correct" after the sentences that contain no errors. Check your answers on page 132. They need not be exactly the same as those supplied, but they should be similar. If you make one mistake, be sure you understand why before going on to the next exercise. If you make more than one mistake, review sections **7c** and **7d** of the *Handbook*.

1. You are getting very sleepy; your eyelids are becoming heavier and heavier; you fell into a deep hypnotic sleep.
2. The man in black walked over, looked him straight in the eye, and says, "Draw!"
3. Off he goes to the racetrack and left his desk covered in unpaid bills.
4. Your responsibilities include locking all doors behind you, and don't let anyone in without a key.
5. Mr. Stevenson was the kind of man who became argumentative whenever he drinks.
6. The employees demanded that, if smoking was to be abolished in the public areas of the building, it be still be allowed in private offices.
7. We were doing our best to look respectable when suddenly, Cousin Ruby shouts out that the mother of the bride is wearing sneakers under her gown.
8. I wish that it was possible to improve graduation rates.
9. If Isaac would have worked harder and taken advice when it was offered, he would very likely have retained his scholarship.
10. Berthenia lacked experience but is willing to work hard to learn.

EFFECTIVE SENTENCES

8 Sentence Unity: Consistency

8a
Making the relationship of ideas in a sentence immediately clear helps the reader.

■ Exercise 8.1
Where possible, rewrite each of the following sentences to make the relationship between its ideas clear. If the ideas cannot reasonably be related in a single sentence, put them in two sentences. Check your answers on pages 132–33. Your answers need not be exactly the same as those supplied, but they should be similar. Consider carefully any of your answers that differ markedly from the sample corrections to see if you can discover weaknesses. Review sections **8–8a** in the *Handbook* if you are in doubt.

1. The moose eats the same sorts of plants as most other members of the deer family, and it is the largest member of the family.
2. I can hardly be expected to work full time at a job that doesn't pay very well and graduate with honours as well.
3. Gardening is a relaxing hobby, but you can eat vegetables and you can only look at flowers.
4. Yasmeen lives far away in Victoria now, and a summer romance is often a memorable experience.
5. He put up a wooden birdhouse, hoping for purple martins and had to have the cast on his leg for nearly three months.
6. The cherry tree looked beautiful after I pruned it, and it was struck by lightning the following week.
7. The real estate agent listed their house in April, but the lawn had more attraction than the house after the fire.
8. In general, you get what you pay for, and yard sales are great for bargains.
9. I like pancakes that taste as if they were just cooked on a griddle, not thawed in a microwave oven, and Uncle Leroy's House of Flapjacks is way over on the other side of town.
10. Babies are one of the most wonderful gifts life has to offer, and where will saving a lot of money get one anyway?

8b
Arranging details in a clear sequence makes your point clear.

■ Exercise 8.2

Improve the following sentences by rearranging details and trimming excessive detail. Check your answers on pages 133–34. Your answers need not be exactly the same as those supplied, but they should be similar. Consider carefully any answers that differ substantially from those supplied to see if you can discover weaknesses in your version. Review section **8b** of the *Handbook* if you are in doubt.

1. The police visited Mr. Aristides, our neighbour, in the green house with white shutters next door, last night, and his rabbits, some black, some white, some black and white with small patches of brown, visited our garden again today.
2. Mrs. Ramirez was advised by the Humane Society that her chihuahua, Toby, a very small dog with comparatively large erect ears, which she had owned for only a few weeks, would, regardless of illustrations in the magazine that had given her the idea of buying him in the first place, prefer not to be placed in a teacup until the tea had been entirely removed.
3. We visited Stanley Park in Vancouver, with its beautiful trees, rose garden, and abundant wildflowers and its zoo and aquarium containing over 6,000 species, last summer.
4. It was his birthday and, dressed in his best jeans and favourite red shirt, which had little denim patches on the pockets that gave it a western look, Jake walked up the cement steps to pick up his sweetheart, hoping she knew, or at least suspected, although he could not be sure, what day it was.
5. As a boy in New Brunswick, it was nothing for Uncle Leo to wade through snow for three kilometres, or even longer if one counts the long driveway to the family farm, in order to get to elementary school and of course later on, high school.
6. During the first week of official spring, which begins on March 21, the young man's thoughts, not unlike the thoughts of thousands and perhaps hundreds of thousands or even millions of young men before him, not of course to mention contemporaries, many of whom also had the same idea, began turning, slowly at first, but then more and more obsessively to romantic matters.
7. Randy discovered found that his bar fridge, which was brown and sat precariously on the small bar he had constructed for himself in his basement recreation room, had for some reason stopped and leaked water all over the carpet.
8. Although all the lots in our neighbourhood now have houses, thirty years ago, there were only three houses across the street from us built by the same builder, although our house wasn't built until later in 1958 for a supermarket executive.

9. The beaver, a comparatively huge aquatic rodent that gnaws up full-grown trees to dam up streams and build lodges with front and back doors underwater where it raises its young, or kits as they are called, is pictured on Canada's nickel.
10. It was a miserable day, wet and cold and rainy, so dreary the cats did nothing but sleep on the couch, refusing to budge even when Aunt Olga accidentally nudged their dish with her foot when she was making headcheese and we kids just stared out the window daydreaming about all the things we could have been doing if the weather had only cleared up and watching the drops of water make trails down the glass.

8c

Mixed metaphors and mixed constructions are illogical.

8d

Faulty predication can lead to problems.

■ Exercise 8.3

Revise the following sentences to eliminate mixed and awkward constructions and faulty predication. Check your answers on page 134. Your answers need not be exactly the same as those supplied, but they should be similar. Consider carefully any answers that differ substantially from those supplied to see if you can discover weaknesses in your version. Review sections **8c** and **8d** of the *Handbook* if you are in doubt.

1. The bicycle path beside the river is invigorating when jogging early in the morning.
2. Buddy was on fire with a burning passion for flying and took to it like a duck takes to water.
3. Because he cannot afford to pay his insurance explains why Ken has put his motorcycle in storage for the school year.
4. Crazy Guy's efforts to break the ice at the party eventually got him in hot water with his hosts.
5. Most of the tourists who visit Lake Ohara in the course of a summer arrive in a bus.
6. A notorious instance of shoddy journalism is the royal family hounded by the British tabloids.
7. The members of the audience were glued to their chairs as the orchestra took them soaring to greater and greater heights.
8. The study showed that over two-thirds of the city's adult residents live in an apartment.

9. Because of Louise's responsibilities as a member of the Police Commission makes it difficult for her to take a long vacation.
10. During her summer vacation in Europe, Andrea was as free as a bird, although she found herself financially strapped on occasion.

8e

Unnecessary shifts are disconcerting.

(1) Faulty *is . . . when*, *is . . . where*, or *is . . . because* constructions

(2) Consistent tense, mood, and person

(3) Consistent person and number (see also 6b)

(4) Shifts between direct and indirect discourse (see also 10a)

(5) Consistent tone and style

(6) Consistent perspective and viewpoint

■ Exercise 8.4

Revise the following sentences to eliminate needless shifts. Check your answers on pages 134–35. If you make one mistake, be sure you understand your error before going on to the next exercise. If you make more than one mistake, review section **8e** of the *Handbook* carefully.

1. While we were driving home from skiing, Fritz wants to listen to music while his older brother insists on hearing the hockey game.
2. I would be very grateful if someone would volunteer to put up the tent, and pound the stakes in all the way this time.
3. The stadium was an architectural marvel; our lockers were dark grey and so poorly lighted that we could barely see our belongings.
4. Where a person learns how to think as opposed to just memorizing facts is true education.
5. As the aerobics lesson progresses and the tempo and difficulty of the exercises increased, he began to think that the instructor was out to humiliate him and tries even harder to keep up.
6. The flood that struck Winnipeg in May destroyed hundreds of homes, businesses, and vehicles, and millions of dollars in damage was caused by it.
7. The Laszlos have always wondered what happened to Polly, and how did she get out of both her cage and the house in the first place?

8. One of your co-workers would help if they knew what was needed.
9. If she were not so busy working toward her law degree and was able to practise regularly, she could be one of the best tennis players in the country.
10. With its epic significance and its intrinsic narrative and historical interest, Exodus has been one of the most influential books of the Bible on subsequent literature, and it has also provided the source for some pretty good flicks as well.

■ Exercise 8.5

Revise the following sentences to eliminate needless shifts. Check your answers on page 135. If you make one mistake, be sure you understand your error before going on to the next chapter. If you make more than one mistake, review section **8e** of the *Handbook* carefully.

1. It is hard to judge if many really well-known writers will be willing to accept the low pay offered by Canada's little magazines and how many will be satisfied with such a small audience?
2. In the evening news, the announcer reported that 24 persons were known to have died in the bombing, and the probable death toll was said by him to be even higher.
3. Clear writing is when what you write can be understood by your readers immediately.
4. I would rather have my meat overcooked than dangerously rare, but somewhere there must have been a reasonable medium.
5. We at the conservatory have always found it stimulating and informative to begin the day with a gab session.
6. The performer was excellent, but the audience becomes progressively more frustrated as the sound system keeps breaking down.
7. The farm spread out for many hundreds of metres in all directions; in spite of the lack of light, we noticed immediately that the potatoes in the cellar were going to seed.
8. We spent the morning setting up the rides for the circus, and in the afternoon, they were tested by us.
9. Both of the paramedics were soon on the scene of the train derailment carrying his medical pack.
10. More climbers fall going down than climbing up for the simple reason that, when one is really tired, that's when you're most likely to make a mistake.

■ Exercise 8.6

Revise the following sentences to eliminate needless shifts. Check your answers on pages 135–36. If you make one mistake, be sure you understand your error before going on to the next exercise. If you make more than one mistake, review section **8e** of the *Handbook* carefully.

1. A jam session is where jazz musicians get together informally and perform improvisations.
2. We watched the buses moving along the highway below the overpass, and it was impossible to see anything out the filthy windows.
3. Everyone get their gear together because we leave in five minutes.
4. Brenda was afraid of mice, but hamsters and gerbils were adored and pampered by her.
5. David Harper just called to say that the twister had taken his father's barn, that he had to go and look for it, and would I please give him a three-day extension on his essay?
6. The passionate precision with which the master played his violin really wowed the audience.
7. The view from their kitchen window was nothing less than inspirational, but the plastic butterflies glued on their roof looked ridiculous.
8. One thing nobody could say about Zach was that he is shy.
9. We believe that the instruction booklet that comes with the camera is clearly worded, so why can't people take decent pictures?
10. Following one's own inclinations will often get you further than if you follow someone else's advice.

9 Subordination and Co-ordination

9a

Careful subordination can combine a series of related short sentences into longer, more effective units.

Ideas inappropriately expressed in main clauses can be subordinated in adjectives and adjective phrases, adverbs and adverb phrases, appositives, and subordinate clauses.

9b

Using subordination and co-ordination is preferable to stringing several main clauses together.

(1) Subordinate structures for ideas that are less important than main ideas

(2) Co-ordinate structures for ideas of equal importance

■ Exercise 9.1

Using effective subordination, rewrite each of the following sentences and groups of sentences as either a single complex or simple sentence. Check your answers on page 136. Your answers need not be exactly the same as those supplied, but they should be similar. Consider carefully any of your answers that differ substantially from those supplied to see if you can discover weaknesses in your version. If you find more than one weak revision, review sections **9**, **9a**, and **9b** of the *Handbook.*

1. Sometimes it is necessary in sports to take a chance in order to have a chance to win. But taking unnecessary chances for thrills is a mistake. Such chances will lead to losing far more often than winning.
2. Andrew went on a rigorous diet. He vowed he would lose enough weight to have the operation on his windpipe. Then he would begin training for the marathon.
3. Summer jobs for students were hard to find this year. A special employment agency for students was created. It was staffed mainly by students.
4. The wendigo is a truly Canadian monster. It belongs to Algonquian mythology. It is cannibalistic.

5. Yesterday I was jogging. It occurred to me that many of the things we do for relaxation are actually tiring. Some are far more taxing than our real work.
6. The winning run was scored by Fernandez. It was a homer. It went into the bleachers in left field.
7. Legend has it that a ghostly pirate ship haunts the Bay of Fundy. It is said to be Captain Kidd's. It is said to appear to frighten those who attempt to find the various treasures Kidd hid there.
8. Last weekend my neighbour dropped by to borrow my hedge trimmer, but I was taking a nap, and he found the trimmer himself in the patio, and then he left a note explaining that he had borrowed it.
9. *David Copperfield* was written in 1849 and 1850. It is one of Charles Dickens's best-loved novels. It is also his most autobiographic.
10. A skinner does not actually skin animals. He is actually a teamster of horses or mules. The term originated in the North American West. It is still in use there.

■ Exercise 9.2

Using effective subordination, rewrite each of the following sentences and groups of sentences as either a single complex or simple sentence. Check your answers on page 137. Your answers need not be exactly the same as those supplied, but they should be similar. Consider carefully any of your answers that differ substantially from those supplied to see if you can discover weaknesses in your version. If you find more than one weak revision, review sections **9**, **9a**, and **9b** of the *Handbook*.

1. I was driving home to Ottawa for the Christmas break. I had a blowout. I was nearly killed.
2. The Salvation Army was founded in England in 1865. William Booth started it. Its purpose is to help unfortunate people and spread the Christian religion. Today, the organization operates in many countries.
3. A police car chased a speeding car down our street last night, and my two cats took refuge in a tree, and then they refused to come down for nearly three hours.
4. The avalanche stopped just short of Alexandros's tent. But Alexandros wasn't even aware of it. He had on headphones. He heard nothing.
5. Pip was apprenticed to Joe. Joe was a blacksmith. But Pip had expectations of being a gentleman. He wasted many years pursuing false ambitions.

6. His head ached. He found he wanted to cough continually. He pushed on with the climb, however. He wanted desperately to reach the summit. He hoped the headache and cough would pass.
7. Phuong is a part-time fireman, and he is paid very little for his work, but he loves the excitement, so he would probably do the work for nothing.
8. Rose accidentally dropped a bottle of perfume into her handbag. She also lost track of three bottles of nail polish from the same place. The store detective accused her of shoplifting.
9. Mr. Lindquist drove the truckload of furniture from Halifax to Sudbury. Mrs. Lindquist went by plane. She disliked driving. She especially disliked driving long distances with Mr. Lindquist.
10. Stephen Leacock is one of Canada's best-known humorists. He is also among the best loved. He was actually born in England. But he came to Canada as a boy.

■ Exercise 9.3

Using effective subordination and co-ordination, rewrite each of the following sentences and groups of sentences as either a single complex, compound, or simple sentence. Check your answers on pages 137–38. Your answers need not be exactly the same as those supplied, but they should be similar. Consider carefully any of your answers that differ substantially from those supplied to see if you can discover weaknesses in your version. If you find more than one weak revision, review sections **9**, **9a**, and **9b** of the *Handbook*.

1. Spring came late this year, July was abnormally dry, and the gardens have suffered.
2. The camp had no plumbing or electricity, the nights were dark and cold and long, and we soon found ourselves longing for such comforts as hot baths and television sets.
3. Mrs. Abernathy's husband died, and she seemed lost without him for almost a year, but then she joined a senior citizens' club, and she is now the president.
4. The blue whale is the largest animal on earth. It is the largest animal that has ever lived on earth. A blue whale can grow to be 30 metres long and weigh 130,000 kilograms. It is larger than the largest dinosaurs.
5. Anook is a science student. His special interest is genetics. He claims it is the science of the future.
6. Taking taxis when one has been drinking can be inconvenient. It can also be expensive. Being convicted of impaired driving is far more inconvenient and expensive.

7. Northrop Frye is probably Canada's best-known literary critic. He is probably also the country's most-respected critic. As a young man, he studied theology and became a United Church minister. His ideas about the Bible as a source of literature have been especially influential.
8. My grandfather was a sceptic by nature. Still, he admitted that a gypsy fortuneteller had once read his mind. She had described in detail the house he had lived in as a small child many years ago.
9. On my grandparent's farm, there are some chickens. My grandparents also keep a few rabbits. But beef cattle are their main concern.
10. We missed the sports scores. We called the radio station. The operator said we would have to wait for the next sportscast.

9c
Faulty or excessive subordination can confuse the reader.

■ Exercise 9.4
Revise the following complex sentences to eliminate excessive or overlapping subordination. Check your answers on page 138. Your answers need not be exactly the same as those supplied, but they should be similar. Consider carefully any answers that differ substantially from those supplied to see if you can discover weaknesses in your version. Review section **9c** of the *Handbook* if you are in doubt.

1. I have known Rolf, whom, even though he lives over 4,000 kilometres away, I feel I can talk to him more openly than many friends whom I see regularly, ever since we were boys in elementary school.
2. Veronica's mother got a traffic ticket for making a left turn without signalling, and, while she explained that her signal light had not been working for some months on the car, which was an old one, because her husband, who was not handy with tools and lazy too, had failed to get the signal fixed, the officer refused to tear it up.
3. With six papers due in a week and his Christmas exams approaching rapidly, Ivan, wanting to do well in all subjects in order to retain his scholarship, which required him to make at least a B on every subject, locked himself in his apartment, unhooked his phone, and painted his windows black so that he would not be distracted by unimportant things like the sun rising and setting.
4. Of the many athletic facilities offered by my university, which were recently upgraded thoroughly, I especially appreciate the

fine indoor track, which is a great convenience in the winter, and the Olympic-size pool, in which I like to swim at least three times a week.

5. My wife and I recently became members of a cottage community that consisted of summer residents who left the city whenever they could to live temporarily by Loon Lake, which represented the natural world that they felt to be missing in their daily lives.
6. Visiting the Victoria Bakery, which is located on Queen Street, which runs parallel to King Street but one block north, Jan was impressed by cookies decorated with British flags and cakes that were shaped to represent Queen Victoria and the Tower of London.
7. When the wind, which was biting and dreadfully cold, blew harder by the hour, sweeping over the plains from the northwest, and the snow continued to fall, drifting higher and higher around the house, we became more and more worried about Theo, who, we of course knew, had started from town in only a light fall jacket, jeans, and sneakers.
8. If she is able to win a scholarship, Consuela, who intends to continue after her undergraduate degree, which she is now taking at Acadia University, which is in Nova Scotia, will study for her doctorate at the University of Toronto.
9. When Mrs. Callihoo, who was teaching the third grade at the time, recently asked her pupils what they wanted to be when they grew up, a little boy named Brent, whose family, so Mrs. Callihoo says, was fairly well-to-do, said he wanted to be a slum landlord because that was where the real money in real estate was.
10. When Mrs. Papadopoulos retired, her employers found, which caused them much dismay, that it was impossible to find anyone with similar experience to replace her, so they carried on without her, and, in time, discovered, which gave them great joy, that the office ran just as well without her.

10 Parallelism

10a
Similar grammatical elements need to be balanced.

10b
Parallels need to be clear to the reader.

Repeating a preposition, an article, the *to* of the infinitive, or the introductory word of a phrase or clause can make parallel structures clear.

10c
Correlatives can be used with parallel structures.

With the correlatives *(both. . . and, either. . . or, neither. . . nor, not only . . . but also, whether. . . or)*, parallel structures are required.

■ Exercise 10.1
Revise the following sentences to correct weaknesses in parallelism. Some sentences may be correct. Check your answers on page 139. If you make one mistake, be sure you understand your error before going on to the next exercise. If you make more than one mistake, review sections **10–10c** of the *Handbook*.

1. The investment consultant told us to avoid uninsured investments, to stay away from real estate for the next two years, and that it would be best to put what we have stuffed in the mattress into a bank.
2. She could climb out of her playpen when she was ten months old, open the back door when she was eighteen months old, climb over the gate when she was two, and now we don't know where she is.
3. All of us grew up, most of us grew old, but only some grew weary.
4. Arnold decided to leave the farm because the city offered better jobs, more varied educational opportunities, a more exciting social life, and his parents finally refused to feed him any more.
5. Madame Zenobia claimed to have been reincarnated as an Egyptian princess, a warhorse in the Middle Ages, a Tibetan lama, and in her last life, she claimed to have appeared as a 1936 Oldsmobile.
6. They knew they were wrong to borrow the car without permission, to drive it at excessive speed over gravel roads, and then leave it far from where they found it.

7. She is one writer with a real dedication to her craft and who is genuinely well read.
8. Candace has gone down the Klondike River in a raft, climbed mountains in the Rockies, and now she is recovering from the fractured hip she received while learning to ride a motorbike in Bermuda.
9. The doctor gave Mr. Bigger a choice of either ether or having a local anesthetic.
10. The kitten located the birds, picked out the one she wanted, but found to her dismay that she was unable to fly.

■ Exercise 10.2

Revise the following sentences to correct weaknesses in parallelism. Some sentences may be correct. Check your answers on pages 139–40. If you make one mistake, be sure you understand your error before going on to the next exercise. If you make more than one mistake, review sections **10–10c** of the *Handbook*.

1. Mr. Gladue is the last person I would expect to see taking ballroom dancing lessons and, in fact, one whom I am surprised to find doing anything physical at all, especially after dark.
2. Student employees are conscientious, hardworking, and they are usually desperate enough to work for the minimum wage.
3. Climbing frozen waterfalls requires strength, steady nerves, knowledge of the proper tools, and it is very important to have clothes that keep you warm and dry, too.
4. In undertaking long-term projects, one is usually motivated either by a desire to accomplish something or by wanting to avoid not accomplishing it.
5. Sabra asked her parents to give her her own phone for Christmas and for her birthday in June, that they pay the long-distance charges she had accumulated.
6. The scouts marched steadily all day, set up camp for the night, and slept soundly until dawn.
7. The ground where they mined thirty years ago is still barren with its slag heaps and which has very little topsoil even today.
8. My alderman claims to have always remained accessible to individual constituents and that he has never sought personal advantage from his political career.
9. Mrs. Cardinal was neither interested in municipal politics nor was she willing to let those who were plant a sign on her front lawn.

10. The inexperienced writer feels awkward when trying to express herself, partly because the act of writing seems unnatural and awkward and speaking seems so natural.

■ Exercise 10.3

Revise the following sentences to correct weaknesses in parallelism. Some sentences may be correct. Check your answers on page 140. If you make any mistakes, review sections **10–10c** of the *Handbook*. If all your answers are correct, skip the next exercise.

1. Whether a child believes in Santa Claus or if he thinks that Santa is just a myth, he will likely enjoy finding presents under his Christmas tree all the same.
2. They planned to rent the canoes by the day, the weekend, or the week, and they had also arranged a plan whereby a customer could apply rent to the purchase price.
3. He seems to have outgrown his hobbies every ten years, starting with mountain climbing when he was fifteen, race car driving when he was twenty-five, and now, at thirty-five, he has given up skydiving.
4. The fire engines raced down Sherbrooke Street and sounding their sirens all the way.
5. In winter, Belinda likes not only to explore back-country trails on skis but also skating.
6. Allan impressed the other scouts with his maturity, his resourcefulness, and by drinking beer from a bottle while standing on his head.
7. There's a time for laughter and also for tears.
8. A good dog can give you companionship, protection, and, if you're not lucky, fleas.
9. Our teacher speculated that Hamlet not only resented his uncle's stealing the throne of Denmark from him but also having his studies interrupted in the middle of the term.
10. She was the dentist we had visited longest in Brantford and whom we liked the best.

■ Exercise 10.4

Revise the following sentences to correct weaknesses in parallelism. Some sentences may be correct. Check your answers on pages 140–41. If you make any mistakes, review sections **10–10c** of the *Handbook* carefully and pay close attention to parallelism when revising your own writing.

1. When driving the Trans-Canada Highway through New Brunswick, one passes by Moncton, Sussex, Jemseg, and then, near Fredericton, begins to follow the Saint John River.
2. The main problems with having a cottage so close to the lake are traffic to and from the water, damage from ice in the winter, and the smaller children have to be watched constantly in case they get into trouble.
3. Bicycling, cross-country skiing, and swimming are his three favourite sports.
4. Imelda had always wanted to be either a queen, an art collector, or to own a shoe store.
5. She has everything it takes to become a great statesperson: intelligence, diplomacy, organizational skill, and she comes across well on television.
6. When selling my car, I found it worthwhile to wash it, vacuum the floor and trunk, and parking it at some distance from the oil stain in my driveway.
7. In graduate school, Tomoko found he liked the intellectual freedom, hated the boring classes, and fearing the prospect of having to write a thesis.
8. Lucky is faithful, obedient, and he will eat almost anything you give him.
9. Three causes of back-country skiing accidents are hidden obstructions, unstable snow, and taking unnecessary risks.
10. For a smooth ride, nothing can beat radial tires, but for holding the road when going around turns at high speed, I prefer regular tires of good quality.

11 Emphasis

11a
Words at the beginning or end of a sentence receive emphasis.

11b
When surrounded by cumulative sentences, a periodic sentence receives emphasis.

11c
When ideas are arranged from least important to most important, the most important idea receives the most emphasis.

11d
Forceful verbs can make sentences emphatic.

(1) The active is more emphatic than the passive voice.

(2) Action verbs and forceful linking verbs are more emphatic than forms of *have* or *be*.

11e
Repeating important words gives them emphasis.

11f
Inverting the standard word order of a sentence gives it emphasis.

11g
Balanced sentence construction provides emphasis.

11h
A short sentence following one or more long ones is emphasized.

■ Exercise 11.1

Identify the primary method or methods of enhancing emphasis in each of the following sentences and groups of sentences. Indicate your choice by placing, after the sentence, the corresponding letter of the section in **Chapter 11** in the *Handbook* in which that method is discussed. (The sections and their appropriate letters have been listed above as well.) Check your answers on page 141. If you make more than one mistake, review the chapter before going on to the next exercise.

1. Feed your children; clothe your children; educate your children; but, above all, talk to your children.

2. No matter how domesticated, the cat is true to its instincts first; no matter how wild, the dog's ruling instinct is to become domesticated.
3. All the children adored Chuckles the Clown.
4. For lighting, for heating, for cooking, even for entertaining ourselves, for nearly everything we do in the home, we depend on electricity.
5. We must never part with the land, repeated the grandfather: the land is our life.
6. Only when one stops to think that more than half of all the people who have ever lived on earth are alive today does one grasp the enormity of the population explosion.
7. Spending on jewellery, spending on cars, spending on entertaining their friends, spending on a large house they could not afford, they should have known that before long, they would spend the family business entirely.
8. A down sleeping bag, freeze-dried food, cooking utensils made of the lightest aluminum—everything in her backpack was designed to keep weight to the absolute minimum.
9. The banks are crumbling. The steps are collapsing. The foundation is exposed. By this time next year, the cottages will begin tumbling into the sea.
10. I can hardly speak too enthusiastically of the work she has done establishing schools in remote villages, in persuading medical personnel to establish clinics in areas where the monetary rewards will be low and the work hard, and in organizing volunteers to teach methods of farming and ways of improving sanitation. She is indeed a miracle worker.

■ Exercise 11.2

Identify primary method or methods of enhancing emphasis in each of the following sentences and groups of sentences. Indicate your choice by placing, after the sentence, the corresponding letter of the section in **Chapter 11** in the *Handbook* in which that method is discussed. Check your answers on page 141. If you make more than one mistake, review the chapter before going on to the next chapter.

1. He came, he saw, he purchased.
2. Those who climbed Everest after Hillary had one very important edge: they knew it could be climbed.
3. Sand in their boots and in their pockets, sand in their hair and on their lips, sand in their clothing, in their closed backpacks, and

even in the food they ate—everywhere, for kilometres and kilometres around, the same endless sand reached to the horizons.

4. We have gone to a good deal of trouble in setting up this program, and so it seems very important, not only to the people it was intended to help but to the workers as well, that the benefits of the program be publicized throughout the community so that people will take full advantage of it. Otherwise, we have wasted our time.
5. If you work hard enough, you work long enough, and you choose something to do for which you have a basic aptitude, success is all but inevitable.
6. In the country, he had never locked his door; in the city, it was locked and barred. In the country, he had rarely encountered strangers; in the city, he rarely saw a face he knew.
7. She devoted her life to helping disadvantaged children.
8. He bought the antique car because it was in excellent condition, because the price was good, and, most of all, because it reminded him of the one he drove when he was seventeen.
9. They had one great advantage that their predecessors had lacked: faith that they were doing the right thing.
10. Fundamental to the way we understand the world is the way we classify the things and experiences we encounter in it.

12 Variety

Varying the kinds of sentences you use can make your writing lively and distinctive. Many writers tend to rely too heavily on a few familiar structures, and the result often seems predictable.

12a

A series of short, simple sentences sounds choppy. (See also 11h.)

■ Exercise 12.1

Rewrite each of the following series of short simple sentences as one long sentence in which ideas are carefully related. Check your answers on pages 141–42. Answers may be correct without matching the sample corrections provided, but they should be similar. Referring to section **12a** of the *Handbook*, if necessary, consider carefully any of your answers that differ substantially from those supplied to see if you can discover weaknesses in your version.

1. Mrs. Laderoute wanted a house with hardwood floors. She looked for one for a long time. Finally she found one.
2. A dramatic monologue is a kind of poem. In the dramatic monologue, only one character speaks. He or she speaks to a silent but implied audience. Often the speaker reveals more than he or she intends.
3. Margaret Atwood is a Canadian novelist. Her book, *The Handmaid's Tale,* was made into a movie. It is a futuristic novel. She won her first Governor General's Literary Award in 1966.
4. Harjinder took up jogging. He ran slowly at first. Steadily he increased his distances. He also ran faster. Now he wins cross-country races. It took him less than a year.
5. Charles Dickens was an influential Victorian novelist. He was concerned with social injustice. His novels reflect that concern.
6. Sir Alexander Mackenzie was the first white man to cross the North American continent. He reached the Pacific Ocean in 1793. He started from Fort Chipewyan and crossed the Rocky Mountains to Bella Coola on the coast.
7. Rubber is made from the juice of the rubber tree. It is elastic. It is not easily penetrated by water or air. It also does not conduct electricity. It is very useful.
8. I intend to buy a mountain bike this summer. Mountain bikes are durable. They will stand rough use. A mountain bike will help me get around quickly on hiking trails.

9. Gold is a chemical element. It is yellow and shiny. It is used extensively in making jewellery. It will not rust.
10. Mrs. Laliberte's budgie escaped last Friday. She knew well that budgies are delicate and incapable of living long outside. She quickly recruited the neighbourhood children. They helped her find it and coax it back inside.

12b

Writing sounds monotonous when too many sentences begin the same way.

(1) Begin with an adverb or an adverbial clause.

(2) Begin with a prepositional phrase or a verbal phrase.

(3) Begin with a sentence connective—a co-ordinating conjunction, a conjunctive adverb, or a transitional expression.

(4) Begin with an appositive, an absolute phrase, or an introductory series. (See 9a.)

■ Exercise 12.2

The following sentences all begin with the subject. Rewrite each sentence to vary this common subject-first form. Check your answers on page 142. Answers may be correct without matching the sample corrections provided, but they should be similar. Consider carefully any of your answers that differ substantially from those supplied to see if you can discover weaknesses in your version. Consult section **12b** in the *Handbook* if you are in doubt.

1. The lecturer immediately captured the attention of her audience even though it was not friendly.
2. He decided he would propose as soon as he landed a permanent job.
3. Tibor reached the drowning woman just as she was losing consciousness.
4. Catherine could not complete her degree on time as a result of her illness.
5. Mr. Cardinal did not report the mysterious depressions in his field because he wanted to avoid publicity.
6. We found a swim in the surf especially invigorating after we had spent a long day lolling around on the hot sand.
7. Sunita decided to move to a residence because her mother kept treating her like a child.

8. We left work early on Friday so as to ensure that we would find a place in the campground.
9. They decided to start their own publishing company in order to ensure that their conspiracy theories reached the public.
10. We walked along the country road in the rain with our clothing getting wetter and dirtier as each car passed.

12c

Stringing simple sentences together to make compound sentences is less effective than experimenting with sentence structure.

(1) Make a compound sentence complex.

(2) Use a compound predicate in a simple sentence.

(3) Use an appositive in a simple sentence.

(4) Use a prepositional or verbal phrase added to a simple sentence.

(5) Use additional conjunctions to increase the compounds in a sentence.

■ Exercise 12.3

Using the methods explained in section **12c** of the *Handbook*, revise the loose, stringy compound sentences below. Check your answers on page 143. Answers may be correct without matching the sample corrections provided, but most should be similar. Consider carefully any of your answers that differ substantially from those supplied to see if you can discover weaknesses in your version. Review section **12c** if you are in doubt.

1. Van Minh practised until he could move his hands very quickly, and he also learned how, at exactly the right moment, to distract the attention of people watching him, but he had no intention of becoming a professional magician.
2. Driving a school bus seems a nerve-wracking job, but I know of several people who drive school buses, and none of them seems extraordinarily calm or patient with adults, but all of them genuinely like children, and no doubt that makes the job easier to stand.
3. The weather was excellent, and everyone was in place for the ceremony, but the groom began losing his nerve at the last minute, and he was prevented from taking flight only by the calming influence of the best man and his vivid recollection of his future father-in-law's gun collection.
4. Lemieux started behind his own net, and he skated the entire length of the ice, and not one member of the opposing team managed to get close to him.

5. We considered moving to an area outside the city, and we found that three hectares of land forty kilometres west cost no more than a lot in the city, and we concluded that the money we saved by having a large garden would pay the cost of the extra gas we used travelling back and forth to work.
6. Magpies do not have pretty voices, and they certainly do not have pleasant manners, but at least they do have pretty feathers.
7. Mr. Cavallo had a new underground sprinkler system installed in his lawn, and he believes it is well worth the price, and he is pleased that it saves time watering his lawn, and he is glad that it allows him to amuse himself surprising the cats that hunt birds in his yard.
8. The ice-cream parlour on Superior Street boasted of over eighty flavours, but it always seemed to be out of the most popular ones, and many of the exotic kinds tended to become old and icy before being sold, so the business was eventually sold to a less ambitious owner.
9. Bulldogs are not pretty, but they are intelligent, and they are also patient and loyal, and owners quickly learn to see beyond the superficial ugliness, and they see only the beautiful canine personality within.
10. Clayton wanted to earn money, but he also wanted to learn a trade, so he joined the army, and he filled out all his aptitude and intelligence tests enthusiastically to see what his trade would be, but he soon learned that he would be trained as an infantryman.

12d

Occasionally using words or phrases to separate subject and verb can vary the conventional subject–verb sequence.

12e

When surrounded by declarative sentences, a question, an exclamation, or a command adds variety.

■ Exercise 12.4

Using the methods explained in **Chapter 12** of the *Handbook*, rewrite each of the groups of sentences below as a single sentence in order to improve structural variety in the paragraph they form. Compare your answer with the samples provided on pages 143–44, and consider the differences, making reference to the *Handbook*, if necessary.

1. Native English drama began about one thousand years ago. It originated in church ceremonies. It played a minor part.

2. It consisted of very limited representations of biblical stories within church services at first. But these gradually became more elaborate.
3. The common people could not understand the Latin of the services. And the basic purpose of these representations was to educate rather than to entertain. The dramatic element was popular. It gradually became more extensive.
4. Priests began to speak parts as opposed to just acting them out while the choir sang. Costumes began to appear in the twelfth century.
5. The basic Christmas and Easter stories were supplemented in the twelfth and thirteenth centuries. The stories of the Old and New Testaments were introduced. Cycles developed covering biblical history.
6. Space required by the sets and the audience forced the plays out into the churchyards. The need for more characters made it necessary to use laymen as actors.
7. English replaced Latin. Entertainment became more important. Edification became less important.
8. Humour became common. Characters and concerns were adapted to reflect daily medieval life.
9. The plays were sponsored by the trade guilds in the fourteenth and fifteenth centuries. The Church had divorced itself from the developing drama. It saw the drama as a symptom of moral decay.
10. But the drama had become too popular for even the Church to suppress successfully.

DICTION

13 Good Usage

13a

Dictionaries provide information beyond the definition of a word.

13b

Most dictionaries label words according to dialectical, regional, or stylistic usage.

13c

Writers consider their audience when selecting words to convey meaning and appropriate tone.

■ Exercise 13.1

Underline any word or phrase below that would be incorrect or inappropriate in formal writing intended for a general audience. Check your answers on page 144. If you make more than one mistake, review sections **13–13c** of the *Handbook* and the **Glossary of Usage** before going on to the next exercise.

1. One night when we were high-tailing it through Alberta, we were stopped by the fuzz who had us mixed up with someone else, and I thought we were going to jail for sure, but we had an alibi and managed to worm our way out of it with just a fine.
2. a highly repetitive style in which anadiplosis, anaphora, epistrophe, and epanalepsis were distractingly common
3. the alabastrine skin of her lower extremities contrasting with her filthy feet
4. Since it was only among the two of us, there were less reasons to be careful about what we said.
5. Ben's folks considered his expulsion from the third grade a bummer.
6. The two drunks left the eatery to exchange buffets in the parking lot.
7. possessing an elicit drug, such as pot
8. Alas and alack, the bony finger of Death had once again pointed at some old geezer in our town.
9. The guys played good, but alright just was not good enough.
10. a salad of tomatoes, carrots, and foliaceous vegetables

■ Exercise 13.2

Underline any word or phrase below that would be incorrect or inappropriate in formal writing intended for a general audience. Check your answers on pages 144–45. If you make more than one mistake, review sections **13–13c** of the *Handbook* and the **Glossary of Usage** before going on to the next exercise.

1. The wedding took place in the A.M., but nobody got any eats until nearly three o'clock in the P.M.
2. Most of the girls in the office were in their early 60s, but they were still spunky enough to mosey across the street for coffee half a dozen times each day.
3. He survived the wreck, but his leg was broke and his head was busted.
4. Loretta's uncle felt that emigrants should not be allowed to come to Canada and snap up all the decent lives because his family had been here for several generations and none of them had been given a decent life yet.
5. Lysosomes and even ribosomes were distinguishable with the new microscope.
6. Childless for eight years of marriage, my aunt and uncle sought advise on how to adapt a baby.
7. They bugged him till he flipped his lid and called the cops.
8. However logical his reasoning may seem, his educational theories were derived from faulty principals.
9. Neither orthogenesis nor the opposing idea of allometry at first seemed readily testable.
10. He thought of poesy as his true calling.

■ Exercise 13.3

Underline any word or phrase below that would be incorrect or inappropriate in formal writing intended for a general audience. Check your answers on page 145. If you make more than one mistake, review sections **13–13c** of the *Handbook* and the **Glossary of Usage** before going on to the next exercise.

1. By the time we showed up, the plug-uglies had polished off all the victuals.
2. Jenson's insistence that the work is positively laden with phonocentric metaphors is no doubt partly a function of his own phonocentrism.
3. drawing pogey—a Canadian art form
4. Freeman's problem was that he was trying to create his feature leads out of headline-ese and to write his featurish stories in hard-news style.

5. I read in the paper where a grandmother put the run to two pit-bulls with a broom.
6. a quote from memory
7. There is nowheres I can think of where it would be liable to rain every day in January accept Vancouver.
8. After working on his computer until nearly 3:00 P.M. without taking a break, Chuck raced to the cafeteria, interfaced with a twelve-inch pizza, and processed it in megabytes.
9. If our Lulubelle married your Buford, then sure as shootin' we'd be kin and than all this feuding could stop.
10. sort of a cranky cuss

14 Exactness

14a

Accurate and precise word choice conveys meaning efficiently.

1) Accuracy is essential.

2) Definitions clarify the precise meanings of words.

3) Connotations enrich meaning.

4) Specific and concrete words are usually stronger than general and abstract ones.

5) Figurative language can contribute to exactness.

14b

Exact word choice requires an understanding of idioms.

14c

Fresh expressions are more distinctive than worn-out ones.

■ Exercise 14.1

Revise the following sentences so as to eliminate or replace with more appropriate substitutes any inexact, unidiomatic, and trite words and expressions. Check your answers on pages 145–46. Your answers will naturally vary somewhat from the sample answers supplied, but they should be similar in most cases. Consider carefully the quality of any of your changes that are substantially different from the suggested ones. Review sections **14a–14c** of the *Handbook* if you find more than two instances of weak revision.

1. Marty was disinterested in history, so he didn't do his homework.
2. Wai-Ho was the smallest boy in junior high, and he at least had the consolation of knowing that his father had grown fifteen centimetres in his late teens.
3. The fish weren't biting his bait at all, but Mr. Watters, who was playing a wading game, remained undisturbed.
4. Earlier to the incident, Claude had been practising self-defiance diligently.
5. Dr. Mandryk strove to reverse the effects of the poison by administering a powerful anecdote.

6. The plant manager's daughter, with whom we went to school, had always thought she was better as us, but we knew we were not inferior than she was.
7. Those opposed to the legislation claimed the minister's simple, knee-jerk reaction had turned the matter into a political football.
8. The new currier service is as quick as a bunny and as solid as a rock.
9. Tanya was active in amateur sports but only in a passive sort of way.
10. Mr. McInnis had learned long ago that a bird in the hand was worth far more than beating around the bush, and not counting his chickens before they were hatched made him as happy as a lark.

■ Exercise 14.2

Revise the following sentences so as to eliminate or replace with more appropriate substitutes any inexact, unidiomatic, and trite words and expressions. Check your answers on page 146. Your answers will naturally vary somewhat from the sample answers supplied, but they should be similar in most cases. Consider carefully the quality of any of your changes that are substantially different from the suggested ones. Review sections **14a–14c** of the *Handbook* if you find more than two instances of weak revision.

1. Dr. Wong was disturbed by the high infant morality rate in the district.
2. Mr. McCready claimed he had been struck by a parked car that had been coming at him very quickly on the wrong side of the street.
3. It was plain to all that the little bundle of joy was a chip off the old block.
4. Several members of the Mt. Logan expedition suffered from attitude sickness.
5. Our host was nice and his food was nice, too.
6. Contrary from all the evidence, Aldo's mother insisted that the teachers were jealous of her son's superior intelligence.
7. While trying to be accepted as just one of the boys, the new plant manager had one too many and passed out.
8. During his trip to Spain, Rudolph enjoyed watching the bulls fight and the flamingo dancers, and his trip was cut short when a robber stabbed him with a staccato.

9. The announcer eluded to the near catastrophe.
10. Needless to say, the moment of truth has come, and it stands to reason that, if the problem of illiteracy among supposedly educated persons is not nipped in the bud the moment it rears its ugly head, if we do not strike while the iron is hot and stop it dead in its tracks, institutionalized ignorance will destroy our society lock, stock, and barrel.

15 Conciseness: Avoiding Wordiness and Needless Repetition

Using words economically is fundamental to writing clearly because unnecessary words or phrases distract readers and blur meaning. Good writers know how to make their points concisely.

15a

Every word should count; words or phrases that add nothing to the meaning should be omitted.

15b

Combining sentences or simplifying phrases and clauses can eliminate needless words.

15c

Repetition is useful only when it improves emphasis, clarity, or coherence. (See also 10b, 11e, and 27b(3).)

15d

Pronouns and elliptical constructions can eliminate needless repetition. (See Chapter 6.)

15e

A clear, straightforward style is preferable to an ornate one.

■ Exercise 15.1

Extract the essential meaning from the following sentences, and then revise the sentences to eliminate wordiness and needless repetition. Check your revisions on page 146. Your answers will naturally vary somewhat from those provided, but they should be similar in most cases. In comparing your answers, note especially whether you have allowed any obvious instance of wordiness or repetition to remain. If your revisions seem wordier than the ones supplied, review sections **15a–15e** of the *Handbook* before going on to the next exercise.

1. The members of the Ethics Committee were planning to make changes that would come into effect in the not too distant future.
2. The explosion completely levelled the house and blew the car that was parked beside the house a distance of nearly fifty metres through the air.

3. Students in their first year at university often become so caught up in the social life that they fail to do the basic essentials necessary to maintain passing grades.
4. The month of December is the time of year when more people buy toys than at any other time of the year.
5. Before doing anything else, the first thing you should begin with when starting to write an essay is finding something to say.
6. In point of fact, the actual reality of the situation dictates that the parking lot be relocated for a distance of three hundred metres to the west.
7. It is incumbent upon Santa Claus to deliver toys at Christmas to the extent that the limited transportation technology he has available allows him to do so.
8. Notwithstanding the fact that we have prepared carefully, there is still a possibility that unforeseen circumstances may arise and cause problems.
9. When writing, you will, with very little question of a doubt, be able to put to use the information contained in a good dictionary.
10. A man by the name of Dr. Warren McCullough will give a talk on the topic of endangered species in our national parks.

■ Exercise 15.2

Extract the essential meaning from the following sentences, and then revise the sentences to eliminate wordiness and needless repetition. Check your revisions on page 147. Your answers will naturally vary somewhat from those provided, but they should be similar in most cases. In comparing your answers, note especially whether you have allowed any obvious instance of wordiness or repetition to remain. If your revisions seem wordier than the ones supplied, review sections **15a–15c** of the *Handbook*.

1. Character traits and mental attitudes may be contributing factors in eroding away an individual's will to succeed in school.
2. But, nevertheless, the general consensus among specialists in the field of educational psychology is that the system is also at fault.
3. Quite obviously, it was definitely, it was absolutely, and it was without a doubt the most exciting car that Uncle Ari had ever had the pleasure to drive.
4. He loved his new car, and during the time he sat behind the steering wheel of his recent acquisition, manoeuvring his prized possession along the highways and byways around the city, he felt entirely caught up in the enjoyment of what he was doing.

5. Beyond the shadow of a doubt, the source of Art's health problems is that he had indulged in the act of overeating for a long period of time.
6. Since you have failed to take the advice given you by me during the course of the course, I have no alternative but to fail you.
7. My cousin Angela experienced a terrible tragedy by fatally drowning just when she had her whole life to look forward to.
8. I feel compelled to make it clear that I do not appreciate the footprints made by your cat's tiny footpads during the early morning when dew and other moisture has accumulated on the surface of my car.
9. There is nothing to be gained by shedding tears over milk which has already been lost from its container.
10. After going to a great deal of personal expense to maintain his old car, Tsui finally decided to make an about-face and to sell it to someone in the neighbourhood for something in the neighbourhood of $600.

16 Clarity and Completeness

16a
Articles, pronouns, conjunctions, or prepositions are sometimes necessary for clarity and completeness.

16b
Verbs and auxiliaries that are sometimes omitted in speech are necessary in writing to avoid awkwardness or to complete meaning.

16c
Complete comparisons are needed in writing to complete the meaning if it is not suggested by the context.

16d
The intensifiers *so, such,* and *too* need a completing phrase or clause.

■ Exercise 16.1
Improve the following sentences by adding the words that have been incorrectly omitted. Check your answers on page 147. If you make more than one mistake, review **16a–16d** of the *Handbook* carefully before going on to the next exercise.

1. The premier's record in his second term was not as good as his first.
2. As soon as he spent one term taking the veterinary course, he knew he had found his true calling in life.
3. José believed the man who was going to buy his old car intended to restore it.
4. What bothered them most was their social worker, who had a very heavy caseload, didn't seem to care about them as human beings.
5. The drive across Ontario took longer than the Prairie Provinces.
6. This information neither contributes nor takes away from our understanding of the situation.
7. I must admit that I have never been fond of that type movie.
8. Rajiv's aggressive behaviour stems the insecurity of his early childhood.
9. Mr. O'Shea has always and always will have a special affection for Ireland even though he has never actually been there.
10. During the summer, Oksana deposited over $4,000 and took only $700 from her account.

■ Exercise 16.2

Improve the following sentences by adding the words that have been incorrectly omitted. Check your answers on pages 147–48. If you make more than one mistake, review **16a–16d** of the *Handbook* carefully before going on to the next exercise.

1. The river had been rising for nearly a week and still continuing to rise steadily.
2. The financial advisor warned Jill Downy, Inc. was about to fall several points.
3. One barrier to becoming a pharmacist these days is that textbooks cost so.
4. Mr. Ponti likes watching television more than Mrs. Ponti.
5. Painting takes longer than vinyl siding.
6. The poem which Professor Popplestone alluded was not in our textbook.
7. If you intend to start your own business, you better consult a lawyer first.
8. Lately I been thinking about moving to Australia where the weather's warm and dry most of the year.
9. They decided renting would be more expensive than a house.
10. That chest drawers you got at the garage sale has no back.

PUNCTUATION

17 The Comma

17a

Commas come before a co-ordinating conjunction that links independent clauses.

17b

A comma usually follows introductory words, phrases, and clauses.

■ Exercise 17.1

Improve the following sentences by adding commas. Do not add unnecessary commas. Some sentences may be correct. Check your answers on page 148. If you make more than one error, review sections **17a** and **17b** of the *Handbook* before going on to the next exercise.

1. Climbing the volcanoes of Mexico provides experience at high altitude but many peaks in the Canadian Rockies are more challenging.
2. It is especially important to do well in your third year at university for admissions lists for many professional schools will be closed by the time the results of the fourth year are available.
3. Although Edmonton is farther north than Edmunston spring comes earlier because much less snow accumulates during the winter and what there is melts much faster in the warm prairie wind than in the thick New Brunswick forest.
4. In fact one sometimes encounters snow in shady places in early summer.
5. Cinderella's gown was expensive and beautifully designed but her glass slippers, though a perfect fit, were still hard on feet long accustomed to going bare.
6. Except in winter encounters with bears are always a possibility for backpackers in the mountain parks but there have been far fewer attacks than encounters.
7. Considering the figures objectively one has to admit that the chances of being attacked by a bear are far slimmer than the chances of being involved in a car accident on the way to the park.
8. Abraham wanted to buy racehorses with his lottery winnings but his financial advisor told him to invest in real estate instead.
9. My present job is boring and doesn't pay well so I intend to join the RCMP as soon as possible.

10. However that may be some time away because many others have the same idea and there is a waiting list.

■ Exercise 17.2

Improve the following sentences by adding commas. Do not add unnecessary commas. Some sentences may be correct. Check your answers on pages 148–49. If you make more than one error, review sections **17a** and **17b** of the *Handbook* carefully.

1. Each independent clause in a compound sentence could stand alone as a complete thought and the point where they come together is normally the most important division in the sentence.
2. The *Journal* kept its archives up to date and stored them in a fireproof vault.
3. Many of the books in the library were very old and rare and some were deteriorating rapidly because of the excessive humidity yet the librarians were told that no money was available to improve conditions.
4. A car compass is inexpensive, easy to install, and simple to adjust and it is an especially worthwhile investment for anyone who expects to drive in unfamiliar cities.
5. The warm, dry fall has allowed farmers to harvest their grain in good condition yet many of them will be lucky to break even because prices are so low.
6. After investing five years of hard work into his business he found himself further in debt than when he started.
7. Researchers are now discovering that much of the stiffness and soreness elderly people experience in their joints results from lack of use and some maintain that regular exercise can make a person feel ten to twenty years younger.
8. Even though the Andromeda Galaxy appears as a mere haze of light in the constellation of the same name it actually contains three hundred billion stars.
9. The galaxy is over two million light-years away so we see it only as it was long before human beings first walked the earth.
10. While tornadoes levelled trees and telephone poles and caused power failures throughout the southern half of the province people in Edmonton felt nothing more than a stiff breeze.

17c

Commas separate items in a series (including co-ordinate adjectives).

17d

Commas set off non-restrictive and other parenthetical elements, as well as contrasted elements, items in dates, and so on.

17e

Commas are occasionally needed for ease in reading.

■ Exercise 17.3

Improve the following sentences by adding commas. Do not add unnecessary commas. Some sentences may be correct. Check your answers on page 149. If you make more than one error, review sections **17c**, **17d**, and **17e** of the *Handbook* before going on to the next exercise.

1. The slapshot wrist shot and backhand shot are a goalie's most easily handled shots. It's the flips scoops and unexplained hops that really put his or her reflexes to the test.
2. When hiking in Central America where you may encounter anti-American feeling it is wise to sew a Canadian flag on your backpack.
3. Green beans spinach and celery are three of the least fattening foods you can eat; cheesecake whipped cream chocolate desserts and cashew nuts are four very highly caloric foods.
4. Wash your face brush your teeth comb your hair and eat your breakfast say mothers all over the world to their kids before sending them off to school.
5. The Senators while losing the series in five played respectably throughout.
6. Can anyone explain the cause behind a sneeze a hiccup or a yawn?
7. Calgary, Alberta was the site of the Winter Olympics in 1988.
8. My second daughter Juliet Elizabeth was born on July 12, 1998.
9. Give me baton twirling tap-dancing and poem reciting and I'll give you a grade three school year closing.
10. "If you want to be writers" asked the famous novelist "why aren't you all home writing?"

■ Exercise 17.4

Improve the following sentences by adding commas. Do not add unnecessary commas. Some sentences may be correct. Check your answers on pages 149–50. If you make more than one error, review sections **17c**, **17d**, and **17e** of the *Handbook* carefully before going on to the next exercise.

1. Most of the students, notwithstanding higher tuition fees hope to return to university in the fall.
2. "You'll need two extractions several fillings a root canal a cleaning and a fluoride treatment" chuckled the dentist.
3. They all tried even the children to return the beached whale to the sea.
4. The rookie marched up to the plate raised the bat to his shoulders spat in the dirt dug in his heels and looked the pitcher straight in the eye.
5. Forty large marshmallows a quarter cup of butter, five cups of Rice Krispies and a teaspoon of vanilla are all you need for Rice Krispies squares.
6. Mount Victoria one of the most photographed mountains in Canada, is located at the western end of Lake Louise.
7. Beautiful though it is Mount Victoria's slopes are prone to avalanching, and a section of Abbot Pass which runs between Victoria and Mount Lefroy its southern neighbour is known locally as "The Death Trap."
8. Throughout the summer months however the pass is generally safe early in the morning when snow still hard from the night's cold is relatively stable.
9. I ordered soup a chicken salad sandwich apple pie with ice cream and being on a strict diet my coffee black.
10. The daffodils tulips and crocuses may be the early bloomers, but I prefer to wait for the sweet-scented roses, sweet peas and lilacs.

■ Exercise 17.5

Improve the following sentences by adding commas. Do not add unnecessary commas. Some sentences may be correct. Check your answers on page 150. If you make any errors, be sure you understand them before going on to the next exercise.

1. When the canola was being planted in the spring there had been no sign of the difficulties that would follow in summer.
2. By the second week of August the grasshoppers had destroyed millions of dollars' worth of crops.
3. Continuing into the fall the plague of grasshoppers devastated the crops.
4. Nevertheless the farmers harvested what they could, applied for crop insurance and began planning for the next year.
5. The play was the funniest in the festival and it had to be because it was also by far the longest.

6. Do we dare choose a restaurant on the advice of a person whose favourite breakfast consists of ketchup and scrambled eggs?
7. The children naturally high-spirited were particularly lively on this occasion.
8. Dr. Vivaldi a leading authority on natural disasters and something of a disaster in his own right attempted to amuse his audience with anecdotes about earthquakes tidal waves, volcanoes, and landslides.
9. Whenever Naissa heard someone mention roses which wasn't very often at the Centre for Arctic Research her thoughts would drift back to her childhood in Victoria.
10. For the widower, Saturday May 16 1987, would remain a day of grief forever.

17f

Unnecessary (or misplaced) commas send false signals that can confuse a reader.

(1) Commas do not separate the subject from its verb or verb from its object.

(2) Commas do not follow co-ordinating conjunctions, and they immediately precede them only when they link independent clauses.

(3) Commas set off only those words and short phrases that are clearly parenthetical.

(4) Commas do not set off restrictive (necessary) clauses, phrases, or appositives.

(5) Commas do not precede the first or follow the last item of a series (including a series of co-ordinate adjectives).

■ Exercise 17.6

Improve the following sentences by removing any unnecessary commas. Some sentences may be correct. Check your answers on page 151. If you make any errors, review section **17f** of the *Handbook*, and be sure you understand your mistakes before going on to the next exercise.

1. We found it difficult to decide, which was the most deserving of the three projects.
2. Even cats that have been pampered and stuffed with the best pet food money can buy, will eat birds and mice.
3. City inspectors traced the chemical spill to a storm drain on the south side, but were unable to find out who was responsible for it.

4. Studies show that the branch offices are understaffed, particularly in personnel trained to operate all but the most basic computer software.
5. It is a mistake to suppose that most students in engineering are there, because they cannot handle arts subjects.
6. The discovery reported in the *Journal of Dead Sea Studies*, will be an extremely important one if it is genuine.
7. The fans clapped enthusiastically as the show began, but, were more subdued by the time it had ended.
8. When we got off the plane in Gander, we found the weather, cold, damp, and foggy.
9. Occasionally an adverb clause will be loosely related to a main clause so that, what is technically a subordinating conjunction, will function much as if it were a co-ordinating conjunction.
10. Although Andy pedalled as fast as he could, the older boys, all of whom had twenty-one speed bikes, gradually left him behind.

■ Exercise 17.7

Improve the following sentences by removing any unnecessary commas. Some sentences may be correct. Check your answers on page 151. If you make any errors, review section **17f** of the *Handbook* carefully, and understand your errors before attempting the next exercise.

1. The scavenger hunters were required to find such challenging things as, horseshoes, opera glasses, and wooden spoons.
2. Not surprisingly, Mount Robson, the highest peak in the Canadian Rockies, is often shrouded in cloud.
3. Mountain goats can reverse direction on a narrow ledge by planting their front feet solidly, and then walking round the wall behind them on their hind feet.
4. Holmes explained, that neither of the two most obvious interpretations was necessarily the correct one.
5. The girl, with braces on her teeth, has a winning smile nonetheless.
6. She claims that the term, *can't*, is not in her vocabulary.
7. After several hours in the waiting room, Mr. Cohen was told, not without suffering mild shock, that his wife had begun to have her babies.
8. As well as local animals, the wildlife park also contained many large, exotic, rarely seen, beasts, the names of which we could sometimes barely pronounce.
9. We travelled to Thunder Bay, but did not have time to visit Sibley Provincial Park.

10. Perhaps, we had better reconsider our itinerary, which may be impractical in the time we have left.

■ Exercise 17.8

Improve the following sentences either by inserting or deleting commas. Some sentences may be correct. Check your answers on pages 151–52. If you make any errors, be sure you understand why before going on to the next chapter.

1. Although bacteria can be seen with a light microscope most of their details are made clear only when they are seen through electron microscopes.
2. In their general overall shape, bacteria appear as, spheres, rods, or spirals.
3. When my Uncle, Mirko, announced his five-year plan for improving the house and yard my cousins began plotting to run away from home.
4. The island, in the middle of the lake, has a sheltered cove on the south side.
5. Realizing that she is not a good listener Juanita attempts to make up for this limitation by being an extremely good talker.
6. The pirates were on the verge of mutiny, when Captain Patch threatened to make the ship's parrot walk the plank.
7. When Mrs. Purdy read about the proposed law requiring, that cats be kept on leashes, she called Mayor Bearspaw to suggest that birds be tied up too.
8. Throughout the ceremony and for days thereafter, her thoughts kept returning to the broom leaning conspicuously against the altar.
9. Moshe lacks experience, but is willing to do almost anything to gain it.
10. Hard work and a willingness to take advice, will usually make a new employee welcome regardless of inexperience.

18 The Semicolon

18a
Semicolons connect independent clauses not linked by a co-ordinating conjunction.

18b
Semicolons separate elements that themselves contain commas.

■ Exercise 18.1
Improve the following sentences either by inserting semicolons where necessary or by replacing commas with semicolons. Some sentences may be correct. Check your answers on page 152. If you make more than one error, review sections **18a** and **18b** of the *Handbook* before going on to the next exercise.

1. Many kinds of fears can lead to insomnia, however, the most common one is the fear of not going to sleep.
2. Notwithstanding the fact that Quebec City is somewhat out of my way, I still intend to visit it.
3. Professor Goblin's Chaucer class bores me, he seems to care more about the language than the literature.
4. The buzzer buzzed, the halls filled with the sound of students changing classes, yet Professor Goblin continued on his pilgrimage.
5. The guest speakers converged on the podium, all at the same time: Biles, the physician, Bounder, the industrialist, Link, the diplomat—all eager to wrest their honorary degrees from the trembling hands of the chancellor and be off.
6. I'm okay, you're okay.
7. Of all the people who have ever lived on earth, half are alive today, of all the people who have ever lived on earth, half are dead.
8. Be prepared, I always say, I'll have a case of each.
9. A study of boredom at work has shown that university professors have comparatively interesting jobs; more interesting than policemen and almost as interesting as medical doctors.
10. Some students today read serious literature, others, who think of reading as merely entertainment, prefer popular fiction, but many others, who have been conditioned to media that require less work than books, prefer to read only the credits following movies and television programs.

■ Exercise 18.2

Improve the following sentences either by inserting semicolons where necessary or by replacing commas with semicolons. Some sentences may be correct. Check your answers on pages 152–53. If you make more than one error, review sections **18a** and **18b** of the *Handbook* carefully before going on to the next exercise.

1. Waldo gathered all the information he could find on the great villains of history, someday he hoped to be one.
2. The language is dead, the literature is very much alive.
3. Professor Marx was sure of his calling: he was a committed scholar, an imperturbable lecturer, and a dedicated bore.
4. It was a cool night, the air was damp; the peepers in the swamp were obviously excited.
5. Go directly to jail, do not pass go, do not collect $200.
6. The guest speakers included an animal trainer, whose greatest achievement was teaching a troupe of turtles to perform a slow, but very elaborate, marching routine, a lady who, having broken with her employer, the SPCA, was opening her own animal shelter, and a trophy hunter, who claimed to have shot everything from hummingbirds to killer whales.
7. The camping trip was an unqualified success: we experienced a classic bear attack, involving a mother and two cubs, we were thoroughly drenched twice, once in a downpour and once when crossing a stream, and we ran out of food, except for raisins and hard candy, two days before we made it back to the parking lot.
8. "The trolls are all ready and outfitted, General Trog, but they say they want a better benefit package, including a dental plan, before they attack."
9. A goat may seem an odd companion, yet, on the other hand, it is one of the easiest pets to feed.
10. I like the house, however, the yard is much too shady.

18c

Semicolons do not connect parts of unequal grammatical rank.

■ Exercise 18.3

Improve the following sentences by adding or deleting semicolons or by changing semicolons to commas or commas to semicolons. Some sentences may be correct. Check your answers on page 153. If you make more than one error, review sections **18a**, **18b**, and **18c** of the *Handbook* carefully before going on to the next exercise.

1. Uncle Max likes to disconcert other drivers; by painting a picture of the front of a truck on the back of his trailer.
2. If I am nominated, I will not run; moreover, if I am elected, I will never go near my office.
3. When I fly, I always ask for a seat over the wing; in case I have to make an emergency exit.
4. History repeats itself; again, and again, and again.
5. Driving across the country, I kept thinking of the pitiful lot of elderly waitresses in truck stops; who no doubt were thinking of the pitiful lot of people driving across the country.
6. Our flight passed over various places I had never seen from the ground: Saskatoon, Saskatchewan, Dauphin, Manitoba, and Wawa and Owen Sound, Ontario.
7. Research now suggests that skin cancer can result from sunburn; sometimes many years after the sunburn occurs.
8. April, our kitten, was abducted by three small children; who held her prisoner in a basement for two days.
9. They very much wanted a cat but couldn't have one because of their father's allergies.
10. Pat cleaned out her refrigerator completely when her in-laws arrived unexpectedly; she called the result a Patpourri.

■ Exercise 18.4

Improve the following sentences by adding or deleting semicolons or by changing semicolons to commas or commas to semicolons. Some sentences may be correct. Check your answers on pages 153–54. If you make more than one error, review sections **18a**, **18b**, and **18c** of the *Handbook* carefully before going on to the next exercise. If you make no mistakes, skip the next exercise in this chapter.

1. Were it entirely up to me; the penalties for fighting during professional hockey games would be much stiffer.
2. Mrs. Boffin claimed her cinnamon buns were truly decadent, they weighed about half a kilo a piece, and half of that was butter; but the customers loved them.
3. Although Monika was the fastest runner; she twisted her ankle during the first lap and rapidly fell behind.
4. Arriving late, they tried to enter the house quietly; although the burglar alarm made that impossible.
5. "The most perfect lawns have only one kind of grass growing on them," claimed Mr. Petrie; surveying his field of hay with pride.

6. Everyone at the party was ecstatic when Jean-Paul arrived wearing his blue suede shoes; his kazoo gripped tightly in his hand.
7. It was a picturesque old farm, but it seemed to produce nothing more than clover and dandelions.
8. Although the children were all intrigued when Uncle Vito began shaving his head; none of them dared to ask him why.
9. Driving through Montreal is always an educational experience, the local drivers are so willing to teach anyone with out-of-province plates a lesson.
10. Our old electric lawn mower is slow but steady, the new gas model is more powerful but also more temperamental.

■ Exercise 18.5

Improve the following sentences by adding or deleting semicolons or by changing semicolons to commas or commas to semicolons. Some sentences may be correct. Check your answers on page 154. If you find errors, make sure you understand them before going on to the next chapter. Consult the *Handbook* if you are in doubt.

1. The plane left half an hour late, still, the service on board was excellent.
2. Sick plants are not pleasant to have around; but at least few people catch diseases from them.
3. Make the most of your environment, get out there and live a lot.
4. Before Mrs. Gomez came home from the hospital, we mowed her lawn; trimmed her hedges; and swept her walkways.
5. Our flight arrived nearly three hours late, the flight we were supposed to connect with was long gone.
6. Professor Moon regaled the expectant mothers with statistics about the surprising prevalence of birth defects: serious cardiovascular disorders, 48 per 10,000 live births, limb deformities, ten per 10,000 live births, cleft palate, fifteen per 10,000 live births, and so on, and on, and on.
7. While nobody could be absolutely certain; all felt that the music store was somewhere nearby in the mall.
8. Mr. Robertson's nervous habit of laughing in serious situations limited his success as a funeral director, on the other hand, he was well liked in the community nonetheless.
9. Our sales manager does most of his business during lunch; which is just as well since his lunches often last the better part of the afternoon.
10. My New Year's resolutions generally last until the holiday is over; and are forgotten when I return to my usual routine.

19 The Apostrophe

19a

The apostrophe shows possession for nouns and indefinite pronouns (*everyone, everybody*).

■ Exercise 19.1

Insert apostrophes in the following phrases where they are needed. Check your answers on page 155. If you make one error, be sure you understand why before going on to the next exercise. If you make two or more errors, review section **19a** of the *Handbook*.

1. the Heaths houses
2. Renées and Renés car
3. my mother-in-laws poodle
4. ones rights
5. Wednesdays child
6. the two dogs bowls
7. the waters edge
8. a dollars worth
9. all the kings horses saddles
10. our drivers licences
11. operators manuals regulations
12. Santas helpers pointed hats
13. this mornings news
14. a days pay
15. Good Queen Besss pirates ships

19b

The apostrophe marks omissions in contractions and numbers.

■ Exercise 19.2

Using apostrophes, form contractions out of the pairs of words below. Check your answers on page 155. If you make one error, be sure you understand why before going on to the next exercise. If you make two or more errors, review section **19b** of the *Handbook*.

1. they are
2. I am
3. should not

4. we will
5. have not
6. will not
7. he will
8. there is
9. would not
10. here is
11. shall not
12. we are
13. can not
14. we would
15. she is

■ Exercise 19.3

Correct any errors in apostrophes in the following list. In some cases, you may have to change a letter or two as well. Some entries may be correct. Check your answers on pages 155–56. If you make one error, be sure you understand why before going on to the next exercise. If you make two or more errors, review sections **19a** and **19b** of the *Handbook*.

1. Workers' Compensation Board
2. In the end, well all say that alls well that ends well.
3. Shakespeares' comedies best lines
4. womens' rights
5. wont want new worker's
6. Mothers' Day
7. Heres looking at you, kid.
8. Were remembering the way we were.
9. an elephants tusks
10. ladies night
11. I fear Ill soon be ill.
12. Couldn't care, Les?
13. childrens' furniture
14. the mens room
15. Dont count you're chickens' prematurely.

19c

The apostrophe and -*s* form certain plurals.

19d

Personal pronouns and plural nouns that are not possessive do not take an apostrophe.

■ Exercise 19.4

Correct any errors in apostrophes in the following sentences. In some cases, you may have to change a letter or two as well. Some sentences may be correct. Check your answers on page 156. If you make one error, be sure you understand why before going on to the next exercise. If you make two or more errors, review sections **19c** and **19d** of the *Handbook.*

1. We got our M.A.s from the same university at the same time, but we never met because we were in different fields.
2. Baby Nicholas is learning to talk the hard way—without *l* s or *th* s.
3. He pronounces his *thunder* s as *nunder* s and just points to the sky to express *lightning*.
4. He also misses his *l* s greatly in two of his favourite words—*slides* and *slurpies*.
5. Their's is the cottage at the west end of the lake.
6. Who's house is the one with the wall made of stone's?
7. "Mind your *p* s and *q* s," my grandmother used to warn me, but I'm sure the phrase wasn't her's originally.
8. Most of the M.P.s from our province are members of the governing party.
9. My computer prints many more symbols—£'s, ¶'s, and ®'s, for example—than my grandfather's Underwood typewriter.
10. My Oldsmobiles body is rusty, but it's engine runs like new.

■ Exercise 19.5

Correct any errors in apostrophes in the following sentences. In some cases, you may have to change a letter or two as well. Some sentences may be correct. Check your answers on page 156. If you make one error, be sure you understand why before going on to the next exercise. If you make two or more errors, review sections **19a–19d** of the *Handbook.*

1. Monas habit of dotting her *i*s with happy faces failed to impress her employers.
2. Its been a long while since I last went bowling, but my friends say that bowlings time has come.

3. Correcting these sentences is more fun than a trip to Disneyland, isnt it?
4. Isnt it too bad that Maliks cars muffler fell off on the way to his wedding?
5. "Ill show you mine if you show me your's," squealed Sergei, clutching his stamp collection to his chest and wiggling his ears enthusiastically.
6. Were all going to the party on New Years Eve at eight oclock in the evening.
7. Whos going to believe thats how a gentlemans supposed to act?
8. Her's were fond memories of Victorias beautiful gardens.
9. Oh, a sailors lifes the life for me.
10. "Youre not going anywhere for awhile," he said, "because your car batterys dead and Ive got to finish putting this engine back together."

■ Exercise 19.6

Correct any errors in apostrophes in the following sentences. In some cases, you may have to change a letter or two as well. Some entries may be correct. Check your answers on pages 156–57. If you make any errors, review sections **19a–19d** of the *Handbook*. If you make no mistakes, go on to the next chapter.

1. This years hockey season started earlier than last years.
2. If youre not listening, you cant know what were planning to do.
3. The flight to Toronto was nearly forty-five minute's late, but at least Aaron's baggage was transferred automatically.
4. Hell try to tell you what you should and shouldnt do, but dont overestimate his wisdom.
5. The cat licked its paws carefully before jumping onto Bess' lap.
6. Their car wouldnt start, so theyre going to drive with their neighbours.
7. Studies have shown that professors jobs are less boring than most.
8. Once were finished here, lets leave whats left for tomorrow.
9. Its well known that their's is faster than ours.
10. I should've loaned her ours because she couldnt get yours out of the box.

20 Quotation Marks

20a

Quotation marks set off direct quotations and dialogue.

20b

Long quotations are indented.

20c

Quotation marks enclose the titles of short works such as stories, essays, poems, songs, episodes of a radio or television series, articles in periodicals, and subdivisions of books.

20d

Used sparingly, quotation marks may enclose words intended in a special or ironic sense.

20e

Overusing quotation marks detracts from readability.

20f

Follow North American printing conventions for using various marks of punctuation with quoted material.

(1) Place the period and the comma within the quotation marks.

(2) Place the colon and the semicolon outside the quotation marks.

(3) Place the question mark, the exclamation point, and the dash within the quotation marks when they apply only to the quoted matter. Place them outside when they do not.

■ Exercise 20.1

Correct any errors associated with quotation marks in the following sentences. Some sentences may be correct. Check your answers on page 157. If you make one error, be sure you understand why before going on to the next exercise. If you make more than one error, review sections **20a–20f** of the *Handbook*.

1. Wordsworth's lyric about being "surprised by joy" appears in many school readers.
2. Bang! You're Dead! shouted wee Tommy, while Aunty Bea felt her angina pectoris returning like a bullet in her chest.
3. "See ya, Daddy", said the toddler sadly as Mr. Slominski left for Kamloops.

4. "Dare I intrude"? Mr. Schiller asked plaintively.
5. "Don't start your "Dare I intrude?" routine," Bert replied, offering him a chair.
6. Rosa told us that "you are going to Geneva this winter."
7. Ross's 'The Painted Door' is one of the most memorable short stories I can remember.
8. The poem "Death of a Young Son by Drowning" from Margaret Atwood's collection "The Journals of Susanna Moodie" ends with the memorable simile, "I planted him in this country / like a flag".
9. According to most guides to writing, a good writer "does not overuse quotation marks."
10. Roland repeated, as if we hadn't heard him the first time, 'The greatest poem of the twentieth century is Pound's "In a Station of the Metro" because it takes so little time to read.'

■ Exercise 20.2

Correct any errors associated with quotation marks in the following sentences. Some sentences may be correct. Check your answers on pages 157–58. If you make one error, be sure you understand why before going on to the next exercise. If you make more than one error, review sections **20a–20f** of the *Handbook*.

1. "Me go out with André?" exclaimed Monique. "That 'wimp'! That 'bore'! That 'drip'! And besides that, he hasn't asked me."
2. According to Pope,

   True ease in writing comes from art, not chance,

   As those move easiest who have learned to dance.
3. In his *Life of Samuel Johnson,* James Boswell quotes Johnson on writing for pay: " 'No man but a blockhead ever wrote except for money.' "
4. Woody explained to the teacher, "My little brother, who is teething, chewed up my homework, and my mother threw it out because she didn't want him to choke on it."
5. Professor Dooley was obsessed with the idea that The "Fall" of the House of Usher was symbolically about autumn.
6. As the spelling suggests, "The Beatles" were not thinking of insects when they chose a name for their musical group.
7. Having failed to borrow a spare tire for his "crippled" truck, Danny was heard to remark that "it was a long road that had no turning."
8. "I've been trying to finish "War and Peace" since I was fourteen," confessed Jason.

9. Professor Edwards was thrilled when his article "The Physical Source of Bunyan's Slough" appeared in the journal "Studies in Literary Geography."
10. "Stand up and be counted", Ms. Rousseau commanded the kindergarten class.

■ Exercise 20.3

Correct any errors associated with quotation marks in the following sentences. Some sentences may be correct. Check your answers on page 158. If you make any errors, review sections **20a–20f** of the *Handbook*. If you make no mistakes, move on to the next chapter.

1. "Let's get down to the "nitty-gritty" issues and put all the "hollow rhetoric" aside," suggested the head negotiator for the union.
2. Tennyson depicts Ulysses in age as one, "Made weak by time and fate, but strong in will."
3. Moby Dick is not actually the main character of Melville's novel "Moby Dick."
4. "A fool at forty is a fool indeed," sniffed Granny Wyatt.
5. Because it is so often anthologized, particularly in school readers, 'David' is probably Earle Birney's best-known poem.
6. *Litotes* is a way of understating something by denying the opposite.
7. "Never a borrower or a lender be" said Aunt Mattie, who had a proverb ready for every occasion.
8. Bookstore managers report that "The Bible" is the most frequently stolen book.
9. It would seem that "Birney's poem The Bear on the Delhi Road is as much about men as bears", remarked Ramesh gravely.
10. "I'll have three litres of two percent and a half litre of cream for Tabby," Mrs. Sanchez told the cow.

21 The Period and Other Marks

21a
Periods punctuate certain sentences and abbreviations.

21b
The question mark occurs after direct (but not indirect) questions.

21c
The exclamation point occurs after an emphatic interjection and after other expressions to show strong emotion, such as surprise or disbelief.

■ Exercise 21.1
Correct any errors in punctuation in the following sentences. Some sentences may be correct. Check your answers on pages 158–59. If you make one mistake, be sure you understand your error before going on to the next exercise. If you make more than one mistake, review sections **21a**, **21b**, and **21c** of the *Handbook*.

1. The captain shouted excitedly from the upper deck, "Abandon ship! Women and children first! Then man the lifeboats!".
2. Mrs. Perrier called to inquire how we were getting along with digging our well?
3. Is it true that a virtual university is offering a three-month correspondence course leading to a Ph.D.
4. The same organization—can you believe it—will make you a saint for $99.95.
5. "Can you really be serious," she asked?
6. "When I was in junior high.," Mabel reminisced, "we had dances in the gym. and I was kissed for the first time while slow dancing on the foul line."
7. Alas, the exclamation point is all too often overworked!
8. Dr. Beluga had sacrificed his chance to be a pool shark in order to become an M.D.
9. The road to the climber's hut on Orizaba, Mexico's highest mountain, runs to a point over three hundred metres —?— higher than the highest mountain in the Canadian Rockies.
10. "Are we feeling better today?," crooned the physician in his best bedside manner.

21d

The colon calls attention to what follows and separates time and scriptural references and titles and subtitles.

■ Exercise 21.2

Improve the following sentences by adding or deleting colons where necessary. Check your answers on page 159. If you make one mistake, be sure you understand your error before going on to the next exercise. If you make more than one mistake, review section **21d** of the *Handbook*.

1. The participants in the local "flab wars" were: The Fit Family Emporium, Club Gristle, The God and Goddess, and The Burning Bod.
2. We'll have to be up with the sun because the bus leaves at 6.45 A.M.
3. "The Rime of the Ancient Mariner" concludes with the following often-quoted lines:

    He went like one that hath been stunned,
    And is of sense forlorn:
    A sadder and a wiser man,
    He rose the morrow morn.
4. The scouts were filled with anticipation when they saw the sign that said: only 12 kilometres more to Athabasca Pass.
5. Just think what the Romans managed to achieve in the line of decadence: without disco, without punk, and without video games.
6. Helena has several ambitions; to run a marathon, to become a trial lawyer, to live somewhere where it never snows, and to remain healthy until she is one hundred.
7. Rev. McKinley based his sermon on Hebrews 11.3: "By faith we understand that the world was created by the word of God, so that what is seen was made out of things which do not appear."
8. As Walter left home for university, his mother shouted after him her favourite piece of advice: "Always remember this: A fool and his money are soon parted."
9. Each passenger is allowed three pieces of luggage: one large case, one medium-size case, and a smaller bag to carry on board.
10. Our flight passed over various places that I had never seen from the ground, such as: Saskatoon, Winnipeg, and Owen Sound.

21e
The dash marks a break in thought, sets off a parenthetical element for emphasis or clarity, and sets off an introductory series.

■ Exercise 21.3
Improve the following sentences by inserting or deleting dashes or by exchanging dashes and other punctuation. Some sentences may be correct. Check your answers on pages 159–60. If you make one mistake, be sure you understand your error before trying the next exercise. If you make more than one mistake, review section **21e** of the *Handbook*.

1. If a person wants to write well, poetry, fiction, or just correspondence, that person must take the time to practise writing.
2. The audience, producers, top-name performers, leading critics, gave the performers a standing ovation.
3. Science and mathematics are required of all engineering students, while English (though not considered a liability in the profession) is optional.
4. Can't act—can't sing—can't dance: are you sure you belong in show business?
5. Rain, food poisoning, bugs, even a visiting skunk—such were the things that made our week in the wild memorable.
6. When one is flying at 12,000 metres, Lake Superior looks like an ocean, but, then, so does the land around it.
7. Canada has at least one sport (hockey) in which it leads the world.
8. Antique farm equipment, old cars, broken appliances, rolls of wire, and tall, grasping weeds all these made traversing their yard an adventure.
9. The sky was clear all the way when I flew across Canada—at least above 10,000 metres.
10. A study of comparative interest in various jobs has shown not too surprisingly that workers on assembly lines find their jobs boring.

21f
Parentheses set off non-essential matter and enclose characters used for enumeration.

21g
Brackets set off interpolations in quoted matter and replace parentheses within parentheses.

21h

The slash occurs between terms to indicate that either term is applicable and also marks line division in quoted poetry.

21i

Ellipsis points (three equally spaced periods) mark an omission from a quoted passage or a reflective pause or hesitation.

■ Exercise 21.4

Correct any errors connected with parentheses, brackets, slashes, and ellipses in the following sentences. Some sentences may be correct. Check your answers on page 160. If you make one mistake, be sure you understand your error before going on to the next exercise. If you make more than one mistake, review sections **21f**, **21g**, **21h**, and **21i** of the *Handbook.*

1. High altitude pulmonary edema often abbreviated HAPE (which is essentially fluid in the air cells of the lungs) is the most dangerous kind of altitude sickness.
2. According to Dr. James A. Wilkerson's *Medicine for Mountaineering,* the chances of an adult getting high altitude pulmonary edema after ascending quickly to 3,700 metres (12,000 feet) is about one in 200 (0.5 percent).
3. Symptoms include tiredness, coughing, shortness of breath, fast heartbeat, and bubbling sounds, rales, in the lungs.
4. "O chestnut tree, great-rooted blossomer, Are you the leaf, the blossom, or the bole (trunk)?" asks Yeats, considering process and change in "Among School Children."
5. "Thus Constance (sic) does make cowards of us all. . ." proclaimed the nervous Hamlet and then froze.
6. When a student attempted to answer an examination question on Coleridge's "The Rime of the Ancient Mariner" without having read the poem, he—she made the mistake of saying, "They then hung Albert Ross [sic] around the mariner's neck."
7. ". . . I desire those politicians who dislike my overture [omission here] that they will first ask the parents of these mortals whether they would not at this day think it a great happiness to have been sold for food at a year old in the manner I prescribe, and thereby have avoided such a perpetual scene of misfortunes as they have since gone through by the oppression of landlords. . ." writes Swift near the end of "A Modest Proposal."
8. "The advantages of deep-breathing exercises cannot be overstressed." [omission] "Consciously increasing the ratio of breaths to steps is also well worthwhile," writes one authority on altitude sickness.

9. "The late 1960s was a great time to be young," reminisced Helmut. "Peace and love abounded, everyone was idealistic, and . . . well, you could get away with all sorts of stuff you can't today."
10. An aged thrush, frail, gaunt, and small,

    . . .

    Had chosen thus to fling his soul
    Upon the growing gloom.

    Thomas Hardy, "The Darkling Thrush"

■ Exercise 21.5

Correct any errors in punctuation in the following sentences. Some sentences may be correct. Check your answers on page 160–61. If you make no mistakes, skip the remaining exercise in this chapter. If you make any errors, be sure you understand them before going on to the next exercise. Consult the *Handbook* if you are in doubt.

1. "Our new line of winterwear has been very warmly received (no pun intended)", boasted the manufacturer.
2. "Hurry" she said! "The sun has been up for hours, and the others have been gone since first light."
3. Black eyes sparkling, hair carefully washed and combed, teeth as clean as crunching dog biscuits could make them, his little tail poised to wag cutely at the slightest provocation; Snooky entered the audition knowing he was the best dog he could be.
4. "Who's cooking breakfast this morning?", came the muffled question from Brad's sleeping bag.
5. "What a beautiful day" exclaimed Vincenzo: "The sky stretches all the way round the horizon."
6. People who normally live at high altitude may develop high altitude pulmonary edema if they descend to a much lower level for one or two weeks [or, of course, more] and then ascend quickly to high altitude.
7. Lindsay, like her parents, came to regard the bowling alley as her "home away from home": she was really "into" bowling.
8. As the summer wore on, Orville found he was asking himself again and again whether being a lifeguard in a wading pool was the challenging occupation he had hoped it would be?
9. "I have been one acquainted with the night / . . . " begins one of Robert Frost's bleaker and more tightly written poems.
10. I hadn't paid for my trip in advance, so I was not greatly disturbed to find that my travel agent had taken a(n unscheduled) trip of her own (to some unspecified destination in South America).

■ Exercise 21.6

Correct any errors in punctuation in the following sentences. Some sentences may be correct. Check your answers on pages 161. If you make any errors, be sure you understand them before going on to the next chapter. Consult the *Handbook* if you are in doubt.

1. Flying over the Prairie Provinces, one can distinguish little more than the different coloured patches of the fields—at least at 12,000 metres, that is.
2. Niggard, skinflint, lickpenny, moneygrubber, tightwad; such names could not distract Mr. Biggs from his ambition to make himself the richest man in the business.
3. Don't just throw your old clothes away: others need them.
4. "You don't think I look too bright, do you"? said Louis, referring, of course, to his new yellow sport coat.
5. When driving in winter, you will be wise to carry emergency supplies, a tool kit, basic replacement parts, emergency candles, something sweet to eat, extra clothing, and a cell phone.
6. After his release from prison, Mugsie found himself—in brisk demand on the talk-show circuit and in lecture halls.
7. Carmine reported that his "Uncle Guido had spent his first day home from his round-the-world, solo voyage reading the personals columns in the local papers and mumbling to himself."
8. Ling had to run to get to her psych. class by 2;30 P.M.
9. Remember this; the lines in the middle of the road are yellow, and the ones on the sides are white.
10. Oddly: the plants that grew best in the garden were the weeds.

MECHANICS

22 Spelling, the Spell Checker, and Hyphenation

22a
Spelling often does not reflect pronunciation.

22b
When words sound alike but have different meanings, the spelling determines the meaning.

22c
Adding a prefix to a base word changes the meaning.

22d
Adding a suffix may require changing the spelling of the base word.

22e
***Ei* and *ie* are often confused.**

22f
Hyphens both link and divide words.

■ Exercise 22.1
Correct the spelling errors in the following list. Some may be correct. Check your answers on page 162. If you make more than one mistake, review **Chapter 22** of the *Handbook* carefully before going on to the next exercise. Add words you miss to your list of words you tend to misspell.

1. tobaco
2. tomatos
3. likelyhood
4. developement
5. dissagrement
6. courageous
7. beginning
8. a yolk of oxes
9. reducate
10. resemblense
11. selfsatisfied
12. in his fortys
13. inosense

14. labratory
15. goverment

■ Exercise 22.2

Correct the spelling errors in the following list. Some may be correct. Check your answers on page 162. If you make more than one mistake, review **Chapter 22** of the *Handbook* carefully before going on to the next exercise. Add words you miss to your list of words you tend to misspell.

1. agruement
2. pasttime
3. archetecture
4. acheivement
5. both mother-in-laws
6. seven year itch
7. quizes
8. criticism
9. criterions
10. a reel eyeopener
11. heffer
12. vacume
13. exlandlord
14. happyer
15. calender

■ Exercise 22.3

The words below are hyphenated as if they appeared at the end of a line of type. Correct the hyphenation errors. Some words may be correct. Check your answers on pages 162. If you make more than one mistake, review section **22f** of the *Handbook* carefully.

1. selfex-
planatory
2. but-
tercup
3. sis-
ter-in-law
4. o-
bey

5. objective-
ly
6. sitt-
ing
7. para-
llel
8. woodpeck-
er
9. pas-
sing
10. mayor-e-
lect

■ Exercise 22.4

Correct the spelling errors in the following sentences. Some may be correct. Check your answers on page 163. If you make more than two mistakes, review **Chapter 22** of the *Handbook* carefully. Add words you miss to your list of words you tend to misspell.

1. "Before dyeing," the famous detective observed, "the count must have placed the mesage in the envelop."
2. Both the print and broadcast mediums co-operated to ecspose the curruption in the sewer and water department.
3. Alot of leafs have been turned on the calender since I saw you last.
4. The self study was aimed at reducing office expences to man-agable levels.
5. After ten prolific years as a playwrite, O'Malley quit and remained quite for quiet a few years.
6. The tempreture in Calgary is undoutedly colder than that off Saint Johns in winter, but, than, its usually hoter in summer.
7. Mr. Blair would have excepted the appointment accept for the problems he anti-cipated in moving his family over seas.
8. Debbie must of made it to shore sense we found her life preserver and her coat in the same place.
9. The headmaster of the school recieved a letter of censor from a group of concerned parents who felt the books he had allowed in the school liberary were undermining the morales of their childern.
10. Gorilla warfare certainly would of been the answer to their problem, but they had nobody to train the troupes.

23 Capitals

23a

Proper names are capitalized and so usually are their abbreviations and acronyms.

23b

Titles of persons that precede the name are capitalized but not those that follow it or stand alone.

23c

In titles and subtitles of books, plays, essays, and other titled works, the first and last words are capitalized, as well as most other words.

23d

The pronoun *I* and the interjection *O* are capitalized.

23e

The first word of every sentence (or of any other unit written as a sentence) and of directly quoted speech is capitalized.

23f

Capitals sometimes indicate emphasis.

23g

Unnecessary capitals are distracting.

■ Exercise 23.1

Capitalize letters in the following words where necessary. Some may be correct. Check your answers on page 163. If you make one mistake, be sure you understand your error before going on to the next exercise. If you make more than one mistake, review **Chapter 23** of the *Handbook* paying special attention to explanations that pertain to your errors.

1. dalhousie university
2. mrs. tymchuk, the mayor
3. freudianism
4. saskatchewan roughriders football team
5. the arctic circle
6. grey cup
7. greenland whale

8. socratic method
9. bird of prey
10. the big dipper
11. the moon
12. morse code
13. digital camera
14. german measles
15. st. francis

■ Exercise 23.2

Change lower-case letters to capitals and capitals to lower-case letters where necessary. Some may be correct. Check your answers on page 163–64. If you make one mistake, be sure you understand your error before going on to the next exercise. If you make more than one mistake, review **Chapter 23** of the *Handbook*.

1. Russian orthodox church
2. Malaria
3. Unicef
4. girl guides of Canada
5. Halley's Comet
6. April fools' day
7. Imperial Order Daughters Of The Empire
8. Marxian
9. Corner brook, Newfoundland
10. the maritimes
11. Richards' *Hope In The Desperate Hour*
12. Memorial park
13. the memorial in the park
14. Saint John river
15. premier Campbell

■ Exercise 23.3

Change lower-case letters to capitals and capitals to lower-case letters where necessary. Check your answers on page 164. If you make any mistakes, review **Chapter 23** of the *Handbook* carefully.

1. "I tell you, I have seen the flying dutchman with my own two eyes," shouted captain Jacobson.

2. "Oh, but I wish I were going to be here to hear the nobel prize winner speak," exclaimed ms. Bertrand.
3. The children in the sunday school did not have complete bibles, just the new Testament and Psalms.
4. Yi-Su intends to go to Graduate School to get her Doctorate.
5. She is transferring from Simon Fraser university to a University in Toronto.
6. While at Loon lake, they caught six Trout and a smallmouth Bass.
7. One of the characters in the Medieval Morality Play *Everyman* is Good Deeds.
8. Professor Kotsopoulos, my favourite English Professor, does not have a Ph.D.
9. Andy will start work driving a Brink's Truck as soon as he finishes school in the spring.
10. Evergreen books on the South Side of the boulevard near the subway station has good deals on Encyclopedias.

24 Italics

24a
Italics identify the titles of separate publications.

24b
Italics identify foreign words and phrases in the context of an English sentence.

24c
Italics identify the names of legal cases.

24d
Italics identify the names of specific ships, satellites, and spacecraft.

24e
Italics indicate words, letters, or figures spoken of as such or used as illustrations, statistical symbols, or the variables in algebraic expressions.

24f
When used sparingly, italics indicate emphasis.

■ Exercise 24.1
Underline any words that should be italicized in the following sentences. You may want to refer to a good dictionary, and since there is some disagreement about which foreign words and phrases should be italicized, you may accept the authority of your dictionary if it disagrees with the answers provided on pages 164–65. If you make one mistake, be sure you understand your error before going on to the next exercise. If you make more than one mistake, review **Chapter 24** of the *Handbook* paying special attention to explanations that pertain to your errors.

1. Even educated native speakers of English will sometimes confuse forms of lay and lie.
2. Starting the day with CTV's Canada AM has become almost a tradition at our house.
3. Many of the more colourful Maritime place names, such as Passamaquoddy and Nepisiguit, are derived from Micmac and Malecite words.
4. One man's de rigueur is another's hoity-toity.

5. Vis-à-vis what?
6. The phrase de profundis—out of the depths—is taken from the opening of the Latin version of Psalm 130.
7. De Profundis is also the title of a prose apologia written by Oscar Wilde in prison.
8. Her favourite fictional subject was the faux pas of the nouveau riche.
9. King Lear is one of Shakespeare's best tragedies.
10. "Bon appétit," Captain Patch was heard to remark while feeding the piranhas.

■ Exercise 24.2

Underline any words that should be italicized in the following sentences. Some sentences may be correct. Check your answers on page 165. If you make any mistakes, review **Chapter 24** of the *Handbook* before going on to the next chapter.

1. Some people prefer to cross their 7's to avoid having them mistaken for 1's.
2. Others find that a crossed 7 looks too much like a 4.
3. C'est la vie!
4. Alden Nowlan's hilarious story "Miracle at Indian River" appears in a collection also called Miracle at Indian River.
5. Of all his stories, it is perhaps the most strikingly a tour de force.
6. Nowlan had been a reporter for the Observer in Hartland, New Brunswick, the general area where the story is set, and he knew his subjects well.
7. Job has been one of the most influential books of the Bible on literature.
8. The television episodes of Star Trek, along with the movies based on the series, have made the starship Enterprise as famous as any real spacecraft.
9. The Spanish word junta, formerly pronounced with an h, has now become Anglicized to the point where it can also be pronounced with a j.
10. The coup d'état was a fait accompli, and the president was being held incommunicado.

25 Abbreviations, Acronyms, and Numbers

25a

Designations such as *Ms.*, *Mr.*, *Mrs.*, *Dr.*, and *St.* appear before a proper name, and those such as *Jr.*, *Sr.*, and *II* appear after.

25b

The names of provinces, countries, continents, months, days of the week, and units of measurement are not abbreviated when they appear in a sentence.

25c

Words such as *Street*, *Avenue*, *Road*, *Park*, and *Company* are abbreviated only when they appear in addresses.

25d

The words *volume*, *chapter*, and *page* are written out when they appear in sentences but abbreviated when they appear in bibliographies and reference lists.

25e

When unfamiliar with an acronym, readers benefit from seeing it spelled out the first time it is used.

25f

Numbers are written in different ways depending on the size of the numbers and the frequency with which they appear.

■ Exercise 25.1

Place a check mark beside the forms below that would be appropriate in formal writing; place an **X** beside those that would be inappropriate. Check your answers on pages 165–66. If you make one mistake, be sure you understand your error before going on to the next exercise. If you make more than one mistake, review **Chapter 25** of the *Handbook* paying special attention to explanations that pertain to your errors.

1. at 21 Athabasca Avenue, Devon, Alberta
2. AIDS
3. 1/2 of the way home
4. seventy-three years old
5. "4 good reasons come to mind," said Mr. Weiner.
6. Grade 2

7. after receiving his B. Comm.
8. a Sr. partner in the firm
9. about 630 B.C.
10. RCMP
11. Chas. Irwin
12. won two million dollars
13. Phase 3
14. CBC
15. June 2nd, 2002

■ Exercise 25.2

Place a check mark beside the forms below that would be appropriate in formal writing; place an **X** beside those that would be inappropriate. Check your answers on page 166. If you make any mistakes, review **Chapter 25** of the *Handbook* paying special attention to explanations that pertain to your errors. Be careful in future when using abbreviations and numbers in your own writing.

1. N.B. Power
2. in Prof. Mayberry's office
3. over three million copies in print
4. Highway 2
5. The Rev. had a bad cold for the memorial service.
6. attendance of three thousand, two hundred, and sixty-one
7. nine A.M.
8. St. Lawrence River
9. working 6 days a week
10. The decision finally came down to Psych. 201 or Phil. 310.
11. The retired Gen. liked to be called by his military title.
12. Ms. B.N. Ramsingh, B.Ed., et al.
13. next Thurs.
14. the second chapt. of the text
15. A.D. Lam, master of arts

ANSWERS

Exercise 1.1

1. was surprised
2. were
3. was
4. strode, raised, swore, and looked
5. will substantially reduce
6. become
7. were deteriorating
8. is boring and pays
9. Will you stay
10. have sometimes encountered

Exercise 1.2

1. evidence
2. area
3. hills
4. Bart
5. you
6. cars
7. villain
8. sailboat
9. birds
10. cheerleaders

Exercise 1.3

1. climbers
2. challenging
3. victims
4. that the chances of being attacked by a bear are far slimmer than the chances of being involved in a car accident on the way to the park
5. grandfather
6. closed
7. worthwhile
8. Toshihiko
9. first
10. editor

Exercise 1.4

1. reliable
2. soup, salad, and ice water
3. visitors
4. member
5. faithful
6. archives
7. site
8. mother
9. indispensable
10. superb

Exercise 1.5

1. noun
2. verb
3. pronoun
4. noun
5. preposition
6. pronoun
7. noun
8. conjunction
9. adjective
10. noun

11. preposition
12. adjective
13. adjective
14. noun
15. verb
16. adverb

Exercise 1.6

1. adverb
2. preposition
3. noun
4. noun
5. verb
6. adjective
7. noun
8. conjunction
9. verb
10. verb
11. adjective
12. noun
13. pronoun
14. verb
15. verb
16. preposition
17. pronoun
18. noun

Exercise 1.7

1. phrase adverb
2. clause adjective
3. clause adverb
4. clause adverb
5. clause noun
6. phrase adjective
7. phrase adjective
8. phrase adjective
9. phrase adverb
10. phrase noun

Exercise 1.8

1. phrase adjective
2. clause adverb
3. clause adverb
4. phrase adverb
5. phrase noun
6. clause adverb
7. phrase adjective
8. phrase adjective
9. phrase adjective
10. phrase noun

Exercise 1.9

1. simple
2. complex
3. simple
4. compound-complex
5. complex
6. compound
7. complex
8. simple
9. compound-complex
10. compound

Exercise 2.1

1. fragment
2. fragment
3. correct
4. fragment
5. correct
6. fragment
7. fragment
8. correct
9. fragment
10. fragment

Exercise 2.2

1. fragment
2. correct
3. fragment
4. fragment
5. fragment
6. fragment
7. correct
8. fragment
9. correct
10. fragment

Exercise 2.3

1. fragment
2. correct
3. fragment
4. fragment
5. correct
6. fragment
7. correct
8. fragment
9. correct
10. fragment

Exercise 3.1

1. steadily, the	comma splice
2. umbrella, it	comma splice
3. admitted "I had	fused sentence
4. rising it	fused sentence
5. correct	
6. guide, "Can	comma splice
7. parkway traffic	fused sentence
8. correct	
9. novelist, however	comma splice
10. problem, on	comma splice

Exercise 3.2

1. dishes then	fused sentence
2. meat, mine AND liver, it	comma splices
3. 3:00 A.M., it	comma splice
4. centimetre, we	comma splice
5. bored, he	comma splice
6. Juan, "he	comma splice
7. glass it	fused sentence
8. 190°C, then	comma splice
9. correct	
10. birds, however	comma splice

Exercise 3.3

1. o'clock, still AND arrived, it	comma splices
2. sport, it	comma splice
3. correct	

4. early it	fused sentence
5. correct	
6. you, after	comma splice
7. again she	fused sentence
8. correct	
9. throat, it	comma splice
10. Santa, I	comma splice

Exercise 3.4

1. May still	fused sentence
2. correct	
3. walks, the	comma splice
4. embarrassing, why	comma splice
5. corner then	fused sentence
6. correct	
7. EITHER grass, warmed OR sun, they	comma splice
8. country, I	comma splice
9. night never	fused sentence
10. warned, "getting	comma splice

Exercise 4.1

1. loudly
2. quickly
3. hungry
4. hungrily
5. nearly
6. surely, good
7. awfully
8. Merrily
9. graceful
10. clearly

Exercise 4.2

1. [terrible]	terribly
2. [well]	good
3. [accurate]	accurately
4. [badly]	bad
5. [Slow but sure]	Slowly but surely OR correct
6. [brightly]	bright OR correct
7. [careful]	carefully
8. [healthily], [good]	healthy, well
9. [Near]	Nearly
10. correct	

Exercise 4.3

1. friendlier
2. most skilful
3. fastest
4. harder
5. most nearly unique
6. worst
7. most brilliant
8. best
9. costliest
10. more nearly correct

Exercise 4.4

1.	[very best]	best
2.	[quick]	quickly
3.	[best]	better
4.	[the most perfect]	perfect
5.	[older]	oldest
6.	[most funniest]	funniest
7.	[more warm]	warmer
8.	correct	
9.	[jovialest]	most jovial
10.	[worst]	worse

Exercise 4.5

1.	[reckless]	recklessly
2.	[better]	best
3.	[soft]	softly
4.	[muchly]	very much
5.	correct	
6.	[bad]	badly
7.	[tight]	tightly
8.	[surely]	sure
9.	[never]	——
10.	[well]	good

Exercise 4.6

1.	[real], [painless]	really, painlessly
2.	[near]	nearly
3.	[affectionate]	affectionately
4.	[sure]	surely
5.	correct	
6.	[internationally]	international

7. [unfair] unfairly
8. correct
9. [darker] darkest
10. [whole-hearted] whole-heartedly

Exercise 5.1

1. Walking slowly, the old gentleman caught up with the young couple.

   OR

   The old gentleman who was walking caught up slowly with the young couple.
2. In spite of their faults, most of us like to speak well of those who have departed from this world.
3. The life of Hagar Shipley, which lasts well into old age, is the subject of Margaret Laurence's *The Stone Angel.*
4. Although Boris delivers papers in the mornings, he makes it to school on time almost every day.
5. The goalie had not found even his pads by the time the game was supposed to start.
6. Fancy Dancer, who had just galloped round the track in record time, was thoroughly rubbed down by the groom.
7. Before long, they were able to change fundamentally and permanently the procedures for hiring casual staff.
8. At the tender age of three, Davy Crockett is supposed to have killed a bear.
9. The motel owner informed us in no uncertain terms that no pets were allowed in the rooms.

   OR correct
10. Mrs. Bates sat in her bedroom in a chair which rocked incessantly.

Exercise 5.2

1. Everyone present knew that to get the injured child to a hospital immediately was essential.
2. correct
3. We purchased a grand piano weighing at least four hundred kilograms from an elderly gentleman.
4. Bonny's husband announced by telephone that she had just given birth to twins.
5. Huge, hairy, and primitive looking, the buffalo bounded after my girlfriend.
6. Pierre bought new outfits that went for $49.95 on special for his dancers.
7. His faded blue jeans were covered with grass stains.
8. The children found a nest made of straw, mud, and string built by birds.
9. These new laws allow anyone whose marriage has broken down to get a divorce in less than three months.

10. Eating spicy foods fast irritates an ulcer.

    OR

    Eating spicy foods irritates an ulcer quickly.

Exercise 5.3

1. After I had fed the dog, put the cat out, and got the coffee machine ready for the morning, it was nearly two hours before I could get to sleep.
2. Drinking four cups of coffee just to wake up, I realized the day was going to be a long one for certain.
3. His Honda's stereo was stolen by thieves who were lurking behind the theatre.
4. Snapping at the air and slobbering freely, the rabid wolf was shot by the warden.
5. After she had finished an assignment and eaten a quick lunch, the bell rang indicating that it was time for the afternoon classes to begin.
6. Because Ali was unable to stand the strain of his job, the psychologist was his last resort.
7. While she was still in the fourth grade, Robin's parents attempted to explain the facts of life to her.
8. I find live theatre most entertaining when it is competently directed.
9. correct
10. Finally, after we had spent what seemed like many hours in the waiting room, the doctor announced that it was yet another false alarm.

Exercise 5.4

1. To become a professional athlete, a person must practise a great deal.
2. To succeed in any endeavour, one must be committed.
3. correct
4. Anyone thinking of investing in real estate must have titles searched before buying.
5. While we were rowing home, a storm came up suddenly.
6. Guided by the directions on the box, one is supposed to be able to assemble the doll's house very quickly.
7. correct
8. After eating even snacks, you should brush your teeth thoroughly.
9. Pedalling his mountain bike at top speed, poor Herman was pursued by the bear.
10. Without showing any emotion whatsoever, the judge handed down the sentence of execution by firing squad.

Exercise 6.1

1. her
2. its

3. their
4. its
5. his
6. its
7. he, his
8. his
9. their
10. their

Exercise 6.2

1. The public address system asked whether anyone had lost his tickets.
2. At the first sight of its idols, the audience surged forward as if it were a living creature.
3. All those competing must be in top physical condition to assure themselves of having a genuine chance.
4. Nobody wants the deficit to grow, but nobody wants to see his (her, his or her, or his/her) taxes raised either.
5. Each swimmer in the pool should know where her (his, his or her, or his/her) buddy is as at all times.
6. No one knows how many hours go into restoring antique furniture until he does it himself (she does it herself).
7. The committee members stood up and applauded to welcome their new chairperson.
8. Each of the three novelists may be said to have developed a voice all her (his, his or her, or his/her) own.
9. The news media did their parts in exposing the problem of political patronage.
10. If the review board decides to roll back wages, our union will appeal its decision.

Exercise 6.3

1. That zebra would look a lot like our pony if it were not for the zebra's stripes.
2. Arbour Day is observed in some provinces by planting trees; this custom seems harmless.
3. The twins gave interesting reports in class this morning, but the reports sounded a lot alike.
4. Only after her mother had been dead for over a year did Corina learn that her mother had been adopted.
5. Li-Ying remembered leaving her parka in a trunk, but she couldn't find the trunk.
6. The dog, which was trained to attack intruders, was left chained in the yard by his master.

7. A park with many shade trees is located in the ravine behind our backyard, and the park is always cool even in the middle of summer.
8. While Marika was helping her mother wash the car, she accidentally sprayed her mother with the hose.
9. The map shows the Hudson's Bay Building as being just west of City Hall.
10. Taking no warm clothing in their packs and only enough food for lunch, they took the fork to the left, and this error in route-finding turned out to be a serious mistake.

Exercise 6.4

1. Inga carefully explained to Amelia that Amelia had put up with far more from her fiancé than any woman ought to.
2. The windows on the taxis are dirty, so the taxis really ought to be washed.
3. The Simons continued to quarrel with the Wongs over the Wongs' dog's barking and the Simons' complaints to the police.
4. Marvin moved away from home last spring; his mother was completely unable to cope with his moving.
5. My mother informs me that parents never stop worrying about their children—no matter how old the children become.
6. The instruction booklet that comes with the camera is carefully worded, so purchasers should have no trouble understanding how to use the camera.
7. Eric finally decided to take his puppy to the veterinarian who had advised him about horse liniment.
8. Leonard's father, an automobile mechanic, found time to teach him how to do basic repairs when Leonard was thirty.
9. Even though he finds a brook trout's bones a nuisance to remove, Serge eats trout whenever he can get them.
10. Waiters have to work nights, of course, but the tips are good, and Rodrigo doesn't seem to mind working nights.

Exercise 6.5

1. correct
2. Depressed prices make it a good time to invest in real estate, and the property is attractive.
3. Amelia and Claudia find going to college in Quebec challenging because they get to practise speaking a different language there.
4. After watching the program about fleas on pets, Marco remarked to Mikos that he thought Mikos ought to have Shaggy treated.
5. Because Martine and her mother are the same size, Martine often borrows her clothing.
6. Otto met Leo in the park when Leo was on his lunch break.
7. The old bear returned to the beaver lodge day after day, but the beavers always managed to elude him.

8. He followed the path on his bicycle in the evening gloom, but driving was made tricky by numerous baseball-size rocks.
9. The handout sheets introducing the course made the dangers of plagiarism very clear.
10. The retired marshal, who had hung up his guns forever, was surprised to find himself approached by the townspeople.

Exercise 6.6

1. whom
2. whom
3. me
4. me
5. whom
6. who
7. me
8. whom
9. whom
10. Whom

Exercise 6.7

1. I
2. whomever
3. whoever
4. Whom
5. me
6. who, who
7. whom
8. Whom
9. she
10. Who

Exercise 6.8

1. his
2. he
3. he
4. I
5. my
6. you and me
7. my
8. your
9. her
10. my

Exercise 6.9

1. you and me
2. Jacob and me
3. whom
4. who
5. their
6. She and I
7. him and me
8. who
9. him
10. whom

Exercise 7.1

1. are
2. is
3. is
4. find
5. call
6. lives, makes
7. are
8. are
9. plays
10. is

Exercise 7.2

1. was
2. is
3. comes
4. lives
5. was
6. is
7. seems
8. were
9. helps
10. was

Exercise 7.3

1. The doctor on duty, not to mention the nurses who were also working in emergency that night, says that it was the worst accident in years.
2. One of the most common complaints of climbers at high altitude is headaches.
3. They, not I, are going to watch the Grey Cup parade this afternoon.
4. correct
5. *The Diviners* by Margaret Laurence is very moving.
6. Being able to afford a swimming pool is one of the things that make work seem worthwhile.
7. The cat, as well as four new kittens, was on the doorstep in the morning.
8. correct
9. Over my door sit that wretched raven and his buddy the crow.
10. Neither Mama Bear nor Papa Bear likes the idea of little blond girls paying uninvited calls.

Exercise 7.4

1. sat
2. saw
3. flooded
4. has sounded
5. lay
6. demanded
7. felt
8. lain
9. to post
10. will give

Exercise 7.5

1. After serving his time, Mugsie left prison a reformed man.
2. Scheele discovered oxygen in 1772, but it had been there all along.
3. The Ruskins had paid for their trip in advance, so they were afraid of losing their vacation when the cruise line went bankrupt.
4. Come in and sit down.
5. As the weeks passed, it became clear to Malcolm that some of the men in the logging camp were prejudiced against university students.
6. Mrs. Singh had been driving for over forty years when she fell asleep at the wheel and came to rest amid the sympathy cards at her local pharmacy.
7. You will need to hurry to catch them now because they have been gone for nearly half an hour.

8. If you had run all the way over here, you would not be late now.
9. Although he was in good shape generally, Ali found that he was not used to all the bending and lifting he was required to do.
10. Because the spring rain has finally begun to fall, the grass is beginning to turn green.

Exercise 7.6

1. had been
2. played
3. will need
4. were
5. have
6. make
7. see
8. had been
9. should
10. went

Exercise 7.7

1. You are getting very sleepy; your eyelids are becoming heavier and heavier; you are falling into a deep hypnotic sleep.
2. The man in black walked over, looked him straight in the eye, and said, "Draw!"
3. Off he went to the racetrack and left his desk covered in unpaid bills.
4. Your responsibilities include locking all doors behind you and not letting anyone in without a key.
5. Mr. Stevenson was the kind of man who became argumentative whenever he drank.
6. The employees demanded that, if smoking were to be abolished in the public areas of the building, it still be allowed in private offices.
7. We were doing our best to look respectable when suddenly, Cousin Ruby shouted out that the mother of the bride was wearing sneakers under her gown.
8. I wish that it were possible to improve graduation rates.
9. If Isaac had worked harder and taken advice when it was offered, he would very likely have retained his scholarship.
10. Berthenia lacked experience but was willing to work hard to learn.

Exercise 8.1

1. a) The moose is the largest member of the deer family, but it eats the same sorts of plants as most other members.

   b) Although the moose eats the same diet as most other members of the deer family, it grows to be much larger.
2. a) I can't work a full-time job and graduate with honours as well, and my job doesn't even pay well.

   b) My full-time job is making it impossible for me to graduate with honours, and the low pay is not worth it.

3. a) Vegetable gardening, which is just as relaxing as growing flowers, is more practical because you can eat the product.

   b) Gardening is a relaxing hobby, and vegetable gardening has the added advantage of producing an edible product.

4. a) Although Yasmeen lives far away in Victoria now, our summer romance remains a memorable experience.

   b) I will always remember Yasmeen even though we had only one summer together and she now lives far away in Victoria.

5. a) He broke his leg putting up a birdhouse for purple martins and had to wear a cast for nearly three months.

   b) The injury he received putting up a birdhouse for purple martins required him to wear a cast for three months.

6. a) The cherry tree looked beautiful after I pruned it, but it was struck by lighting after only a week.

   b) Even though it looked beautiful when I was done, the time I spent pruning the cherry tree was wasted because it was struck by lightning the following week.

7. a) After they put their house up for sale last April, it was entirely destroyed by fire.

   b) They had their house listed with a real estate agent in April, but a fire left them only the lot to sell.

8. a) While you generally get only what you pay for in stores, yard sales are a different matter.

   b) In general, you only get what you pay for, but yard sales are an exception and can sometimes yield great bargains.

9. a) Although Uncle Leroy's House of Flapjacks is on the other side of town, the old-fashioned pancakes served there make the trip worthwhile.

   b) It's too bad Uncle Leroy's House of Flapjacks is way over on the other side of town because it has excellent pancakes—pancakes that taste as if they were just cooked on a griddle, not thawed in a microwave oven.

10. a) Babies are one of the most wonderful gifts life has to offer and well worth the expense involved in raising them.

    b) Although caring for a baby can be costly, babies are a wonderful gift and well worth the expense.

Exercise 8.2

1. In spite of the warning from the police last night, our neighbour's rabbits were in our garden again today.
2. The Humane Society told Mrs. Ramirez not to put her chihuahua in teacups that contained tea.
3. Last summer, we visited the zoo, aquarium, and the gardens of Vancouver's beautiful Stanley Park.

4. On his birthday, dressed in his best jeans and a western shirt, Jake went to see his girlfriend, hoping she knew what day it was.
5. It was nothing for my Uncle Leo from New Brunswick to wade through snow for three kilometres to get to elementary school.
6. In spring, the young man began thinking more and more about love.
7. Randy discovered that the bar fridge in his recreation room had stopped working and soaked the carpet.
8. Before our house was built in 1958, this neighbourhood consisted of only the three houses across the street.
9. A beaver, sitting on its lodge above the water, is pictured on Canada's nickel.
10. The cold rain kept us children indoors with Aunt Olga and her dozing cats, so we wasted the day staring out the window and daydreaming of better weather.

Exercise 8.3

1. Jogging along the bicycle path beside the river is invigorating early in the morning.
2. Buddy loved flying and found it easy to learn.
3. Because he cannot afford to pay his insurance, Ken has put his motorcycle in storage for the school year.
4. Crazy Guy went too far in attempting to liven up the party and offended his hosts.
5. Most of the tourists who visit Lake Ohara in the summer arrive in buses.
6. A notorious instance of shoddy journalism is the hounding of the royal family by reporters from British tabloids.
7. The members of the audience were caught up in the orchestra's performance.
8. The study showed that over two-thirds of the city's adult residents live in apartments.
9. Louise's responsibilities as a member of the Police Commission make it difficult for her to take a long vacation.
10. During her summer vacation in Europe, Andrea enjoyed being as free as her limited budget would allow.

Exercise 8.4

1. While we were driving home from skiing, Fritz wanted to listen to music while his older brother insisted on hearing the hockey game.
2. I would be very grateful if someone would volunteer to put up the tent, and if that volunteer would be careful to pound the stakes in all the way.
3. The stadium as a whole was an architectural marvel, but down in the locker rooms, our lockers were dark grey and so poorly lighted that we could barely see our belongings.
4. True education is the process of learning how to think as opposed to just memorizing facts.

5. As the aerobics lesson progressed and the tempo and difficulty of the exercises increased, he began to think that the instructor was out to humiliate him and tried even harder to keep up.
6. The flood that struck Winnipeg in May destroyed hundreds of homes, businesses, and vehicles and caused millions of dollars in damage.
7. The Laszlos have always wondered what happened to Polly and how she got out of both her cage and the house in the first place.
8. Your co-workers would help if they knew what was needed.
9. If she were not so busy working toward her law degree and were able to practise regularly, she could be one of the best tennis players in the country.
10. With its epic significance and its intrinsic narrative and historical interest, Exodus has been one of the most influential books of the Bible on subsequent literature, and it has provided the source for some excellent feature films as well.

Exercise 8.5

1. It is hard to judge if many really well-known writers will be willing to accept the low pay offered by Canada's little magazines and whether many will be satisfied with such a small audience.
2. In the evening news, the announcer reported that twenty-four persons were known to have died in the bombing and that the death toll would probably be even higher.
3. Clear writing is writing that can be understood immediately.
4. I would rather have my meat overcooked than dangerously rare, but somewhere there must be a reasonable medium.
5. We at the conservatory have always found it stimulating and informative to begin the day with discussion.
6. The performer was excellent, but the audience became progressively more frustrated as the sound system kept breaking down.
7. The farm spread out for many hundreds of metres in all directions. But for the moment, we were in the dark potato cellar, more concerned with the fact that the potatoes were going to seed than with the view outside.
8. We spent the morning setting up the rides for the circus, and in the afternoon, we tested them.
9. Both of the paramedics, carrying their medical packs, were soon on the scene of the train derailment.
10. More mountain climbers fall going down than climbing up for the simple reason that human beings are more likely to make mistakes when tired than when fresh.

Exercise 8.6

1. A jam session is a gathering of jazz musicians who get together informally to perform improvisations.

2. We watched the buses moving along the highway below the overpass and speculated that it must have been impossible to see anything out the filthy windows.
3. All of you get your gear together because we leave in five minutes.
4. Brenda was afraid of mice, but she adored and pampered hampsters and gerbils.
5. David Harper just called to say that the twister had taken his father's barn, that he had to go and look for it, and that he hoped I would give him a three-day extension on his essay.
6. The passionate precision with which the master played his violin greatly impressed the audience.
7. The view from their kitchen window was nothing less than inspirational; however, from the outside, their house looked ridiculous because they had glued plastic butterflies on their roof.
8. One thing nobody could say about Zach was that he was shy.
9. We believe that the instruction booklet that comes with the camera is clearly worded, so we find it difficult to understand why people using the camera cannot take good pictures.
10. Following one's own inclinations will often get one further than if one follows someone else's advice.

Exercise 9.1

1. Although it is sometimes necessary in sports to take a chance in order to win, taking unnecessary chances for thrills is a mistake because it will lead to losing more often than winning.
2. Vowing he would lose enough weight to have the operation on his windpipe and then begin training for the marathon, Andrew went on a rigorous diet.
3. A special employment agency staffed mainly by students was created this summer to help students search for scarce summer jobs.
4. The cannibalistic wendigo of Algonquian mythology is a truly Canadian monster.
5. When I was jogging yesterday, it occurred to me that many of the things we do for relaxation are actually more taxing than our work.
6. Fernandez's homer into the left-field bleachers was the winning run.
7. Legend has it that Captain Kidd's ghostly pirate ship haunts the Bay of Fundy, appearing to frighten those who seek the various treasures he hid there.
8. While I was napping last weekend, my neighbour borrowed my hedge trimmer, leaving a note to let me know that he had it.
9. Written in 1849 and 1850, *David Copperfield* is one of Charles Dickens's best-loved novels and also one of his most autobiographic.
10. The term "skinner," which originated in the North American West where it is still in use, refers to a teamster of horses or mules and has nothing to do with actually removing hides.

Exercise 9.2

1. I was nearly killed last Christmas when I had a blowout while driving home to Ottawa for the Christmas break.
2. The Salvation Army, which was founded by William Booth in England in 1865 to spread the Christian religion and help unfortunate people, operates in many countries today.
3. After a police car chased a speeder down my street last night, my two cats refused to leave the tree where they had taken refuge for nearly three hours.
4. Because he was wearing headphones, Alexandros heard nothing of the avalanche that nearly struck his tent.
5. Pip was apprenticed to Joe, a blacksmith, but he wasted many years pursuing the illusory dream of becoming a gentleman.
6. Hoping his cough and headache would pass, he pushed on with the climb because he desperately wanted to reach the summit.
7. Phuong, who is more interested in the excitement than the modest pay involved, would probably remain a part-time fireman for nothing.
8. When Rose accidentally dropped a bottle of perfume and three bottles of nail polish into her handbag, the store detective accused her of shoplifting.
9. Although Mr. Lindquist was driving the truckload of furniture from Halifax to Sudbury, Mrs. Lindquist went by plane because she disliked driving long distances with her husband.
10. Stephen Leacock, who is one of Canada's best-known and best-loved humorists, actually emigrated from his native England as a boy.

Exercise 9.3

1. The gardens have suffered from a late spring and an abnormally dry July.
2. Without plumbing or electricity, we found ourselves longing for such comforts as hot baths and televisions during the long, dark, cold nights in the camp.
3. After a year of feeling lost without her dead husband, Mrs. Abernathy joined the senior citizens' club of which she is now president.
4. Growing up to 30 metres in length and weighing up to 130,000 kilograms, the blue whale is the largest animal that has ever lived on earth—larger even than the largest dinosaurs.
5. Anook is studying genetics and claims it is the science of the future.
6. Although taking taxis when one has been drinking can be inconvenient and expensive, it is much less so than being convicted of impaired driving.
7. At one time a student of theology and a United Church minister, Northrop Frye, who is probably Canada's best-known and most-respected critic, has been especially influential in dealing with the Bible as a source of literature.
8. Although my grandfather was a sceptic by nature, he admitted that a gypsy fortuneteller had once read his mind and described in detail the house where he had lived as a small child many years before.

9. Although they have some chickens and a few rabbits on their farm, my grandparents' main concern is raising beef cattle.
10. After missing the sports scores, we called the radio station only to be told that we would have to wait for the next sportscast.

Exercise 9.4

1. I have known Rolf ever since we were boys in elementary school, and, even though he lives over 4,000 kilometres away, I feel I can talk to him more openly than many friends I see regularly.
2. Veronica's mother got a traffic ticket for making a left turn without signalling. She told the officer that it was her husband's fault because, being lazy and not handy with tools anyway, he had left the signal unfixed for months. The officer, however, refused to tear up the ticket.
3. Ivan had six papers due in a week, and his Christmas exams were approaching rapidly. He needed to make at least a B on every subject in order to retain his scholarship. His solution was to lock himself in his apartment, to unhook his phone, and to paint his windows black so that he would not be distracted from his work by unimportant things like the sun rising and setting.
4. Our university's athletic facilities were recently upgraded thoroughly. I especially like the fine indoor track, which is a great convenience in winter, and I also swim in the Olympic-size pool at least three times a week.
5. My wife and I recently became members of a cottage community at Loon Lake. Like the other summer residents, we went to the lake whenever we could to be closer to nature than our everyday life in the city allowed.
6. At the Victoria Bakery, Jan was impressed by the cookies decorated with British flags and cakes shaped to represent Queen Victoria and the Tower of London. The bakery is located on Queen Street, which is one block north of King.
7. The wind, sweeping over the plains from the northeast, was biting and dreadfully cold and blowing harder by the hour. The snow continued to fall, drifting higher and higher around the house. As the storm grew worse, we became more and more worried about Theo, who we knew had started from town in only a light fall jacket, jeans, and sneakers.
8. Consuela is now completing her undergraduate degree at Acadia University in Nova Scotia. If she is able to win a scholarship, she will study for her doctorate at the University of Toronto.
9. Mrs. Calihoo recently posed the familiar question to her third grade students: What do you want to be when you grow up? A little boy named Brent, whose family was fairly well-to-do, said he wanted to be a slum landlord because that was where the real money in real estate was.
10. When Mrs. Papadopoulos retired, her employers were dismayed to find that it was impossible to find anyone with similar experience to replace her. They decided to carry on without her, and, in time, were pleased to discover that the office ran just as well in her absence.

Exercise 10.1

1. The investment consultant told us to avoid uninsured investments, to stay away from real estate for the next two years, and to put what we have stuffed in the mattress into a bank.
2. She could climb out of her playpen when she was ten months old, open the back door when she was eighteen months old, and climb over the gate when she was two, and now we don't know where she is.
3. All of us grew up, most of us grew old, but only some of us grew weary.
4. Arnold decided to leave the farm because the city offered better jobs, more varied educational opportunities, and a more exciting social life and because his parents finally refused to feed him any more.
5. Madame Zenobia claimed to have been reincarnated as an Egyptian princess, a warhorse in the Middle Ages, a Tibetan lama, and, in her last life, a 1936 Oldsmobile.
6. They knew they were wrong to borrow the car without permission, to drive it at excessive speed over gravel roads, and then to leave it far from where they found it.
7. She is one writer who has a real dedication to her craft and who is genuinely well-read.
8. Candace has gone down the Klondike River in a raft and climbed mountains in the Rockies, but now she is recovering from the fractured hip she received while learning to ride a motorbike in Bermuda.
9. The doctor gave Mr. Bigger a choice of either a local anesthetic or ether.
10. correct

Exercise 10.2

1. correct
2. Student employees are conscientious, hardworking, and, usually, desperate enough to work for the minimum wage.
3. Climbing frozen waterfalls requires strength, steady nerves, and knowledge of the proper tools, and it is also very important to have clothes that keep you warm and dry.
4. In undertaking long-term projects, one is usually motivated either by a desire to accomplish something or by a need to avoid not accomplishing it.
5. For Christmas, Sabra asked her parents to give her her own phone and, for her birthday in June, she asked them to pay the long-distance charges she had accumulated.
6. correct
7. The ground where they mined thirty years ago is still barren, with slag heaps and very little topsoil even today.
8. My alderman claims that he has always remained accessible to individual constituents and that he has never sought personal advantage from his political career.

9. Mrs. Cardinal was neither interested in municipal politics nor willing to let those who were plant a sign on her front lawn.
10. The inexperienced writer feels awkward when trying to express herself, partly because the act of writing seems unnatural and awkward and partly because speaking seems so natural.

Exercise 10.3

1. Whether a child believes in Santa Claus or thinks that Santa is just a myth, he will likely enjoy finding presents under his Christmas tree all the same.
2. correct
3. He seems to have outgrown his hobbies every ten years, starting with mountain climbing when he was fifteen, race car driving when he was twenty-five, and now, at thirty-five, skydiving.
4. The fire engines raced down Sherbrooke Street, sounding their sirens all the way.
5. In winter, Belinda likes not only skating but also exploring back-country trails on skis.
6. Allan impressed the other scouts with his maturity, his resourcefulness, and his ability to drink beer from a bottle while standing on his head.
7. There's a time for laughter and also a time for tears.
8. correct
9. Our teacher speculated that Hamlet not only resented his uncle's stealing the throne of Denmark from him but also was bothered about having his studies interrupted in the middle of the term.
10. She was the dentist whom we had visited longest in Brantford and the one we liked the best.

Exercise 10.4

1. When driving the Trans-Canada Highway through New Brunswick, one passes by Moncton, Sussex, and Jemseg and then, near Fredericton, begins to follow the Saint John River.
2. The main problems with having a cottage so close to the lake are traffic to and from the water, damage from ice in the winter, and the necessity of watching the smaller children constantly in case they get into trouble.
3. correct
4. Imelda had always wanted to be either a queen, an art collector, or the owner of a shoe store.
5. She has everything it takes to become a great statesperson: intelligence, diplomacy, organizational skill, and a good television presence.
6. When selling my car, I found it worthwhile to wash it, to vacuum the floor and trunk, and to park it at some distance from the oil stain in my driveway.
7. In graduate school, Tomoko found he liked the intellectual freedom, hated the boring classes, and feared the prospect of having to write a thesis.

8. Lucky is faithful and obedient, and he will eat almost anything you give him.
9. Three causes of back-country skiing accidents are hidden obstructions, unstable snow, and unnecessary risk taking.
10. correct

Exercise 11.1

1. c
2. g
3. d
4. b
5. a
6. f
7. e
8. b, a
9. c
10. h

Exercise 11.2

1. c
2. a
3. e
4. h
5. b
6. g
7. d
8. c
9. a
10. f

Exercise 12.1

1. After a long search, Mrs. Laderoute finally found a house she liked with hardwood floors.
2. A dramatic monologue is a poem in which a single character speaks to a silent but implied audience, often revealing more than he or she intends.
3. Canadian novelist Margaret Atwood, whose futuristic book *The Handmaid's Tale* was made into a movie, won her first Governor General's Literary Award in 1966.
4. Although he started running only a year ago, Harjinder has increased his distances and pace steadily to the point where he now wins cross-country races.
5. The novels of Charles Dickens, an influential Victorian novelist, reflect his concern with social injustice.
6. In 1793, Sir Alexander Mackenzie travelled from Fort Chipewyan across the Rocky Mountains to Bella Coola on the Pacific coast, and he thus became the first white man to cross the North American continent.
7. Made from the juice of the rubber tree, rubber is especially useful because it is elastic, not easily penetrated by water or air, and a non-conductor of electricity.
8. Mountain bikes are durable enough to stand rough use, and I intend to buy one this summer so I can get around quickly on hiking trails.
9. Because it is yellow, shiny, and will not rust, the chemical element gold is used extensively in making jewellery.

10. When her budgie escaped last Friday, Mrs. Laliberte, knowing well that budgies are too delicate to live outside for long, quickly recruited the neighbourhood children to find it and coax it back inside.

Exercise 12.2

1. a) Even though her audience was not friendly, the lecturer captured its attention immediately.

   b) A skilled orator, the lecturer captured her audience's attention immediately even though it was unfriendly.

2. a) So it was settled: as soon as he had landed a permanent job, he would propose.

   b) As soon as he had landed a permanent job, he decided, he would propose.

3. a) Just as she was losing consciousness, Tibor reached the drowning woman.

   b) Not a moment too soon, Tibor reached the drowning woman just as she was losing consciousness.

4. a) Consequently, with the delay caused by her illness, Catherine could not complete her degree on time.

   b) Because of her illness, Catherine could not complete her degree on time.

5. a) Wanting to avoid publicity, Mr. Frost did not report the mysterious depressions in his field.

   b) His aversion to publicity overcoming his curiosity, Mr. Frost did not report the mysterious depressions in his field.

6. a) After a long day lolling around on the hot sand, we found a swim in the surf especially invigorating.

   b) An especially invigorating experience after a long day of lolling around on the hot sand, a plunge in the surf was just what we needed.

7. a) Feeling that her mother kept treating her like a child, Sunita decided to move to a residence.

   b) Because her mother kept treating her like a child, Sunita decided to move to a residence.

8. a) Determined to find a place in the campground, we left work early on Friday.

   b) Because we wanted to be certain to find a place in the campground, we left work early on Friday.

9. a) So that their conspiracy theories would reach the public, they decided to start their own publishing company.

   b) Determined to get their conspiracy theories to the public, they decided to start their own publishing company.

10. a) Walking along the country road in the rain, we found our clothing getting wetter and dirtier as each car passed.

    b) With each car that passed us as we walked along the country road in the rain, our clothing was getting wetter and dirtier.

Exercise 12.3

1. Although Van Minh had no intention of becoming a professional magician, he practised until he could move his hands very quickly and learned how, at exactly the right moment, to distract the attention of his audience.
2. While the people I know who do the potentially nerve-wracking job of driving school buses are not extraordinarily calm or patient with adults, they all genuinely like children, which no doubt makes the job easier to stand.
3. With the weather excellent and everyone in place for the ceremony, the groom began losing his nerve and was prevented from taking flight only by the calming influence of the best man and his vivid recollection of his future father-in-law's gun collection.
4. Starting from behind his own net, Lemieux skated the entire length of the ice without a member of the opposing team getting close to him.
5. When considering moving to an area outside the city, we found that three hectares forty kilometres west would cost no more than a city lot and concluded that having a large garden would save enough to pay for the extra gas we would use travelling back and forth to work.
6. While magpies do not have pretty voices or pleasant manners, they at least have pretty feathers.
7. Mr. Cavallo thinks the underground sprinkler system he has had installed in his lawn is well worth the price because it saves him time watering and lets him surprise the cats that hunt birds on his lawn.
8. Although it boasted of over eighty flavours, the ice-cream parlour on Superior Street always seemed to be out of the most popular ones and allowed many of the exotic kinds to become old and icy while they were waiting to be sold. The business was eventually sold to a less ambitious owner.
9. Owners of bulldogs, which make up for their physical ugliness with intelligence, patience, and loyalty, quickly learn to see beyond the surface to the beautiful canine personality within.
10. Clayton, who had joined the army to learn a trade while being paid, filled out all his aptitude tests enthusiastically, only to learn that he would be trained as an infantryman.

Exercise 12.4

1. Native English drama originated as a very minor part of church ceremonies about one thousand years ago.
2. At first, it consisted of very limited representations of biblical stories within church services, but these soon became more elaborate.
3. Although the basic purpose was to educate the common people, who could not understand the Latin of the services, the dramatic element was popular from the start and over time, became more extensive.
4. Priests began to speak parts as opposed to just acting them out while the choir sang, and by the twelfth century, costumes had begun to appear.

5. During the twelfth and thirteenth centuries, the basic Christmas and Easter stories were supplemented by stories from the Old and New Testaments, and these stories eventually came to form cycles covering biblical history.
6. Space required by the sets and the audience forced the plays out into the churchyards, while the need for more characters made it necessary to use laymen as actors.
7. English replaced Latin, and entertainment replaced edification as the primary goal.
8. As characters and concerns were adapted to reflect daily medieval life, humour became common.
9. By the fourteenth century, the Church, viewing the developing drama as a symptom of moral decay, had divorced itself entirely from it, and plays were sponsored by the trade guilds.
10. The drama had become too popular for even the Church to suppress successfully.

Exercise 13.1

1. One night when we were high-tailing it through Alberta, we were stopped by the fuzz who had us mixed up with someone else, and I thought we were going to jail for sure, but we had an alibi and managed to worm our way out of it with just a fine.
2. a highly repetitive style in which anadiplosis, anaphora, epistrophe, and epanalepsis were distractingly common
3. the alabastrine skin of her lower extremities contrasting with her filthy feet
4. Since it was only among the two of us, there were less reasons to be careful about what we said.
5. Ben's folks considered his expulsion from the third grade a bummer.
6. The two drunks left the eatery to exchange buffets in the parking lot.
7. possessing an elicit drug, such as pot.
8. Alas and alack, the bony finger of Death had once again pointed at some old geezer in our town.
9. The guys played good, but alright just was not good enough.
10. a salad of tomatoes, carrots, and foliaceous vegetables

Exercise 13.2

1. The wedding took place in the A.M., but nobody got any eats until nearly three o'clock in the P.M.
2. Most of the girls in the office were in their early 60s, but they were still spunky enough to mosey across the street for coffee half a dozen times each day.
3. He survived the wreck, but his leg was broke and his head was busted.
4. Michelle's uncle felt that emigrants should not be allowed to come to Canada and snap up all the decent lives because his family had been

here for several generations and none of them had been given a decent life yet.

5. Lysosomes and even ribosomes were distinguishable with the new microscope.
6. Childless for eight years of marriage, my aunt and uncle sought advise on how to adapt a baby.
7. They bugged him till he flipped his lid and called the cops.
8. However logical his reasoning may seem, his educational theories were derived from faulty principals.
9. Neither orthogenesis nor the opposing idea of allometry at first seemed readily testable.
10. He thought of poesy as his true calling.

Exercise 13.3

1. By the time we showed up, the plug-uglies had polished off all the victuals.
2. Jenson's insistence that the work is positively laden with phonocentric metaphors is no doubt partly a function of his own phonocentrism.
3. drawing pogey—a Canadian art form
4. Freeman's problem was that he was trying to create his feature leads out of headline-ese and to write his featurish stories in hard-news style.
5. I read in the paper where a grandmother put the run to two pitbulls with a broom.
6. a quote from memory
7. There is nowheres I can think of where it would be liable to rain every day in January accept Vancouver.
8. After working on his computer until nearly 3:00 P.M. without taking a break, Chuck raced to the cafeteria, interfaced with a twelve-inch pizza, and processed it in megabytes.
9. If our Lulubelle married your Buford, then sure as shootin' we'd be kin and than all this feuding could stop.
10. sort of a cranky cuss

Exercise 14.1

1. Marty was not interested in history, so he didn't do his homework.
2. Wai-Ho was the smallest boy in junior high, but he at least had the consolation of knowing that his father had grown fifteen centimetres in his late teens.
3. The fish weren't biting, but Mr. Watters waited patiently.
4. Before the incident, Claude had been practising self-defence diligently.
5. Dr. Mandryk strove to reverse the effects of the poison by administering a powerful antidote.
6. The plant manager's daughter, with whom we went to school, had always thought she was better than us, but we knew we were not inferior to her.

7. Those opposed to the legislation claimed the minister's hasty reaction had helped create the controversy.
8. The new courier service is fast and reliable.
9. Tanya was involved in amateur sports although he did not play himself.
10. Mr. McInnis prided himself on taking nothing for granted.

Exercise 14.2

1. Dr. Wong was disturbed by the high infant mortality rate in the district.
2. Mr. McCready claimed he had collided with a car parked on the wrong side of the street.
3. The baby clearly resembled her father.
4. Several members of the Mt. Logan expedition suffered from altitude sickness.
5. Our host was charming and entertaining, and he was also an excellent cook.
6. Contrary to all the evidence, Aldo's mother insisted that the teachers were jealous of her son's superior intelligence.
7. While trying to gain acceptance from his employees, the new plant manager drank himself into unconsciousness.
8. During his trip to Spain, Rudolph enjoyed watching the bullfights and flamenco dancers, but his trip was cut short when a robber stabbed him with a stiletto.
9. The announcer alluded to the near catastrophe.
10. It is important to society that all educated persons be truly literate.

Exercise 15.1

1. The Ethics Committee would soon effect changes.
2. The explosion levelled the house and threw a car parked beside it nearly fifty metres.
3. University freshmen often become so caught up in the social life that they fail.
4. December is the busiest month for toy stores.
5. The first step in writing an essay is finding something to say.
6. The parking lot must be moved three hundred metres to the west.
7. Santa Claus should deliver as many toys as he can with a sleigh and eight reindeer.
8. Although we have prepared carefully, problems can still occur.
9. A writer needs a good dictionary.
10. Dr. Warren McCullough will talk about endangered species in our national parks.

Exercise 15.2

1. Personality can limit success in school.
2. However, most educational psychologists agree that the system is also at fault.
3. Uncle Ari loved the car.
4. He loved his new car and thoroughly enjoyed driving it.
5. Art's health problems clearly stem from overeating.
6. Because you have ignored my advice, I have to fail you.
7. My cousin Angela died young by drowning.
8. I don't like your cat leaving footprints on my car.
9. It is no use crying over spilled milk.
10. Because his old car proved too expensive to maintain, Tsui sold it for about $600.

Exercise 16.1

1. The premier's record in his second term was not as good as it was in his first.
2. As soon as he had spent one term taking the veterinary course, he knew he had found his true calling in life.
3. José believed that the man who was going to buy his old car intended to restore it.
4. What bothered them most was that their social worker, who had a very heavy caseload, didn't seem to care about them as human beings.
5. The drive across Ontario took longer than crossing the Prairie Provinces.
6. This information neither contributes to nor takes away from our understanding of the situation.
7. I must admit that I have never been fond of that type of movie.
8. Rajiv's aggressive behaviour stems from the insecurity of his early childhood.
9. Mr. O'Shea has always had and always will have a special affection for Ireland even though he has never actually been there.
10. During the summer, Oksana deposited over $4,000 in and took only $700 from her account.

Exercise 16.2

1. The river had been rising for nearly a week and was still continuing to rise steadily.
2. The financial advisor warned Jill that Downy, Inc. was about to fall several points.
3. One barrier to becoming a pharmacist these days is that textbooks cost so much.
4. Mr. Ponti likes watching television more than Mrs. Ponti does.
5. Painting takes longer than putting on vinyl siding.

6. The poem to which Professor Popplestone alluded was not in our textbook.
7. If you intend to start your own business, you had better consult a lawyer first.
8. Lately I have been thinking about moving to Australia where the weather's warm and dry most of the year.
9. They decided renting would be more expensive than buying a house.
10. That chest of drawers you got at the garage sale has no back.

Exercise 17.1

1. Climbing the volcanoes of Mexico provides experience at high altitude, but many peaks in the Canadian Rockies are more challenging.
2. It is especially important to do well in your third year at university, for admissions lists for many professional schools will be closed by the time the results of the fourth year are available.
3. Although Edmonton is farther north than Edmunston, spring comes earlier because much less snow accumulates during the winter and what there is melts much faster in the warm prairie wind than in the thick New Brunswick forest.
4. In fact, one sometimes encounters snow in shady places in early summer.
5. Cinderella's gown was expensive and beautifully designed, but her glass slippers, though a perfect fit, were still hard on feet long accustomed to going bare.
6. Except in winter, encounters with bears are always a possibility for backpackers in the mountain parks, but there have been far fewer attacks than encounters.
7. Considering the figures objectively, one has to admit that the chances of being attacked by a bear are far slimmer than the chances of being involved in a car accident on the way to the park.
8. Abraham wanted to buy racehorses with his lottery winnings, but his financial advisor told him to invest in real estate instead.
9. My present job is boring and doesn't pay well, so I intend to join the RCMP as soon as possible.
10. However, that may be some time away because many others have the same idea and there is a waiting list.

Exercise 17.2

1. Each independent clause in a compound sentence could stand alone as a complete thought, and the point where they come together is normally the most important division in the sentence.
2. correct
3. Many of the books in the library were very old and rare, and some were deteriorating rapidly because of the excessive humidity, yet the librarians were told that no money was available to improve conditions.

4. A car compass is inexpensive, easy to install, and simple to adjust, and it is an especially worthwhile investment for anyone who expects to drive in unfamiliar cities.
5. The warm, dry fall has allowed farmers to harvest their grain in good condition, yet many of them will be lucky to break even because prices are so low.
6. After investing five years of hard work into his business, he found himself further in debt than when he started.
7. Researchers are now discovering that much of the stiffness and soreness elderly people experience in their joints results from lack of use, and some maintain that regular exercise can make a person feel ten to twenty years younger.
8. Even though the Andromeda Galaxy appears as a mere haze of light in the constellation of the same name, it actually contains three hundred billion stars.
9. The galaxy is over two million light-years away, so we see it only as it was long before human beings first walked the earth.
10. While tornadoes levelled trees and telephone poles and caused power failures throughout the southern half of the province, people in Edmonton felt nothing more than a stiff breeze.

Exercise 17.3

1. The slapshot, wrist shot, and backhand shot are a goalie's most easily handled shots. It's the flips, scoops, and unexplained hops that really put his or her reflexes to the test.
2. When hiking in Central America, where you may encounter anti-American feeling, it is wise to sew a Canadian flag on your backpack.
3. Green beans, spinach, and celery are three of the least fattening foods you can eat; cheesecake, whipped cream, chocolate desserts, and cashew nuts are four very highly caloric foods.
4. Wash your face, brush your teeth, comb your hair, and eat your breakfast say mothers all over the world to their kids before sending them off to school.
5. The Senators, while losing the series in five, played respectably throughout.
6. Can anyone explain the cause behind a sneeze, a hiccup, or a yawn?
7. Calgary, Alberta, was the site of the Winter Olympics in 1988.
8. My second daughter, Juliet Elizabeth, was born on July 12, 1998.
9. Give me baton twirling, tap-dancing, and poem reciting, and I'll give you a grade three school year closing.
10. "If you want to be writers," asked the famous novelist, "why aren't you all home writing?"

Exercise 17.4

1. Most of the students, notwithstanding higher tuition fees, hope to return to university in the fall.

2. "You'll need two extractions, several fillings, a root canal, a cleaning, and a fluoride treatment," chuckled the dentist.
3. They all tried, even the children, to return the beached whale to the sea.
4. The rookie marched up to the plate, raised the bat to his shoulders, spat in the dirt, dug in his heels, and looked the pitcher straight in the eye.
5. Forty large marshmallows, a quarter cup of butter, five cups of Rice Krispies, and a teaspoon of vanilla are all you need for Rice Krispies squares.
6. Mount Victoria, one of the most photographed mountains in Canada, is located at the western end of Lake Louise.
7. Beautiful though it is, Mount Victoria's slopes are prone to avalanching, and a section of Abbot Pass which runs between Victoria and Mount Lefroy, its southern neighbour, is known locally as "The Death Trap."
8. Throughout the summer months, however, the pass is generally safe early in the morning when snow, still hard from the night's cold, is relatively stable.
9. I ordered soup, a chicken salad sandwich, apple pie with ice cream, and, being on a strict diet, my coffee black.
10. The daffodils, tulips, and crocuses may be the early bloomers, but I prefer to wait for the sweet-scented roses, sweet peas, and lilacs.

Exercise 17.5

1. When the canola was being planted in the spring, there had been no sign of the difficulties that would follow in summer.
2. By the second week of August, the grasshoppers had destroyed millions of dollars' worth of crops.
3. Continuing into the fall, the plague of grasshoppers devastated the crops.
4. Nevertheless, the farmers harvested what they could, applied for crop insurance, and began planning for the next year.
5. The play was the funniest in the festival, and it had to be because it was also by far the longest.
6. correct
7. The children, naturally high-spirited, were particularly lively on this occasion.
8. Dr. Vivaldi, a leading authority on natural disasters and something of a disaster in his own right, attempted to amuse his audience with anecdotes about earthquakes, tidal waves, volcanoes, and landslides.
9. Whenever Naissa heard someone mention roses, which wasn't very often at the Centre for Arctic Research, her thoughts would drift back to her childhood in Victoria.
10. For the widower, Saturday, May 16, 1987, would remain a day of grief forever.

Exercise 17.6

1. We found it difficult to decide which was the most deserving of the three projects.
2. Even cats that have been pampered and stuffed with the best pet food money can buy will eat birds and mice.
3. City inspectors traced the chemical spill to a storm drain on the south side but were unable to find out who was responsible for it.
4. correct
5. It is a mistake to suppose that most students in engineering are there because they cannot handle arts subjects.
6. The discovery reported in the *Journal of Dead Sea Studies* will be an extremely important one if it is genuine.
7. The fans clapped enthusiastically as the show began but were more subdued by the time it had ended.
8. When we got off the plane in Gander, we found the weather cold, damp, and foggy.
9. Occasionally an adverb clause will be loosely related to a main clause so that what is technically a subordinating conjunction will function much as if it were a co-ordinating conjunction.
10. correct

Exercise 17.7

1. The scavenger hunters were required to find such challenging things as horseshoes, opera glasses, and wooden spoons.
2. correct
3. Mountain goats can reverse direction on a narrow ledge by planting their front feet solidly and then walking round the wall behind them on their hind feet.
4. Holmes explained that neither of the two most obvious interpretations was necessarily the correct one.
5. The girl with braces on her teeth has a winning smile nonetheless.
6. She claims that the term *can't* is not in her vocabulary.
7. correct
8. As well as local animals, the wildlife park also contained many large, exotic, rarely seen beasts, the names of which we could sometimes barely pronounce.
9. We travelled to Thunder Bay but did not have time to visit Sibley Provincial Park.
10. Perhaps we had better reconsider our itinerary, which may be impractical in the time we have left.

Exercise 17.8

1. Although bacteria can be seen with a light microscope, most of their details are made clear only when they are seen through electron microscopes.

2. In their general, overall shape, bacteria appear as spheres, rods, or spirals.
3. When my Uncle Mirko announced his five-year plan for improving the house and yard, my cousins began plotting to run away from home.
4. The island in the middle of the lake has a sheltered cove on the south side.
5. Realizing that she is not a good listener, Juanita attempts to make up for this limitation by being an extremely good talker.
6. The pirates were on the verge of mutiny when Captain Patch threatened to make the ship's parrot walk the plank.
7. When Mrs. Purdy read about the proposed law requiring that cats be kept on leashes, she called Mayor Bearspaw to suggest that birds be tied up too.
8. correct
9. Moshe lacks experience but is willing to do almost anything to gain it.
10. Hard work and a willingness to take advice will usually make a new employee welcome regardless of inexperience.

Exercise 18.1

1. Many kinds of fears can lead to insomnia; however, the most common one is the fear of not going to sleep.
2. correct
3. Professor Goblin's Chaucer class bores me; he seems to care more about the language than the literature.
4. correct
5. The guest speakers converged on the podium, all at the same time: Biles, the physician; Bounder, the industrialist; Link, the diplomat—all eager to wrest their honorary degrees from the trembling hands of the chancellor and be off.
6. I'm okay; you're okay.
7. Of all the people who have ever lived on earth, half are alive today; of all the people who have ever lived on earth, half are dead.
8. Be prepared, I always say; I'll have a case of each.
9. A study of boredom at work has shown that university professors have comparatively interesting jobs—more interesting than policemen and almost as interesting as medical doctors. (Some writers would use a colon instead of the dash.)
10. Some students today read serious literature; others, who think of reading as merely entertainment, prefer popular fiction; but many others, who have been conditioned to media that require less work than books, prefer to read only the credits following movies and television programs.

Exercise 18.2

1. Waldo gathered all the information he could find on the great villains of history; someday he hoped to be one.

2. The language is dead; the literature is very much alive.
3. correct
4. It was a cool night; the air was damp; the peepers in the swamp were obviously excited.
5. Go directly to jail; do not pass go; do not collect $200.
6. The guest speakers included an animal trainer, whose greatest achievement was teaching a troupe of turtles to perform a slow, but very elaborate, marching routine; a lady who, having broken with her employer, the SPCA, was opening her own animal shelter; and a trophy hunter, who claimed to have shot everything from hummingbirds to killer whales.
7. The camping trip was an unqualified success: we experienced a classic bear attack, involving a mother and two cubs; we were thoroughly drenched twice, once in a downpour and once when crossing a stream; and we ran out of food, except for raisins and hard candy, two days before we made it back to the parking lot.
8. correct
9. correct
10. I like the house; however, the yard is much too shady.

Exercise 18.3

1. Uncle Max likes to disconcert other drivers by painting a picture of the front of a truck on the back of his trailer.
2. correct
3. When I fly, I always ask for a seat over the wing in case I have to make an emergency exit.
4. History repeats itself, again, and again, and again. (For a different stylistic effect, the first comma could also be omitted or changed to a dash.)
5. Driving across the country, I kept thinking of the pitiful lot of elderly waitresses in truck stops, who no doubt were thinking of the pitiful lot of people driving across the country.
6. Our flight passed over various places I had never seen from the ground: Saskatoon, Saskatchewan; Dauphin, Manitoba; and Wawa and Owen Sound, Ontario.
7. Research now suggests that skin cancer can result from sunburn, sometimes many years after the sunburn occurs.
8. April, our kitten, was abducted by three small children, who held her prisoner in a basement for two days.
9. correct
10. correct

Exercise 18.4

1. Were it entirely up to me, the penalties for fighting during professional hockey games would be much stiffer.

2. Mrs. Boffin claimed her cinnamon buns were truly decadent; they weighed about half a kilo a piece, and half of that was butter, but the customers loved them.
3. Although Monika was the fastest runner, she twisted her ankle during the first lap and rapidly fell behind.
4. Arriving late, they tried to enter the house quietly although the burglar alarm made that impossible. (Some writers would put a comma after *quietly*.)
5. "The most perfect lawns have only one kind of grass growing on them," claimed Mr. Petrie, surveying his field of hay with pride.
6. Everyone at the party was ecstatic when Jean-Paul arrived wearing his blue suede shoes, his kazoo gripped tightly in his hand.
7. correct
8. Although the children were all intrigued when Uncle Vito began shaving his head, none of them dared to ask him why.
9. Driving through Montreal is always an educational experience; the local drivers are so willing to teach anyone with out-of-province plates a lesson.
10. Our old electric lawn mower is slow but steady; the new gas model is more powerful but also more temperamental.

Exercise 18.5

1. The plane left half an hour late; still, the service on board was excellent.
2. Sick plants are not pleasant to have around, but at least few people catch diseases from them.
3. Make the most of your environment; get out there and live a lot.
4. Before Mrs. Gomez came home from the hospital, we mowed her lawn, trimmed her hedges, and swept her walkways.
5. Our flight arrived nearly three hours late; the flight we were supposed to connect with was long gone.
6. Professor Moon regaled the expectant mothers with statistics about the surprising prevalence of birth defects: serious cardiovascular disorders, 48 per 10,000 live births; limb deformities, ten per 10,000 live births; cleft palate, fifteen per 10,000 live births; and so on, and on, and on.
7. While nobody could be absolutely certain, all felt that the music store was somewhere nearby in the mall.
8. Mr. Robertson's nervous habit of laughing in serious situations limited his success as a funeral director; on the other hand, he was well liked in the community nonetheless.
9. Our sales manager does most of his business during lunch, which is just as well since his lunches often last the better part of the afternoon.
10. My New Year's resolutions generally last until the holiday is over and are forgotten when I return to my usual routine.

Exercise 19.1

1. the Heaths' houses
2. Renée's and René's car
3. my mother-in-law's poodle
4. one's rights
5. Wednesday's child
6. the two dogs' bowls
7. the water's edge
8. a dollar's worth
9. all the king's horses' saddles
10. our driver's licences
11. operator's manual's regulations
12. Santa's helpers' pointed hats
13. this morning's news
14. a day's pay
15. Good Queen Bess's pirates' ships

Exercise 19.2

1. they're
2. I'm
3. shouldn't
4. we'll
5. haven't
6. won't
7. he'll
8. there's
9. wouldn't
10. here's
11. shan't
12. we're
13. can't
14. we'd
15. she's

Exercise 19.3

1. correct
2. In the end, we'll all say that all's well that ends well.
3. Shakespeare's comedies' best lines
4. women's rights
5. won't want new workers
6. Mother's Day
7. Here's looking at you, kid.
8. We're remembering the way we were.
9. an elephant's tusks
10. ladies' night
11. I fear I'll soon be ill.
12. correct

13. children's furniture
14. the men's room
15. Don't count your chickens prematurely.

Exercise 19.4

1. We got our M.A.'s from the same university at the same time, but we never met because we were in different fields.
2. Baby Nicholas is learning to talk the hard way—without *l*'s or *th*'s.
3. He pronounces his *thunder*'s as *nunder*'s and just points to the sky to express *lightning*. (*thunders* and *nunders* also correct)
4. He also misses his *l*'s greatly in two of his favourite words—*slides* and *slurpies*.
5. Theirs is the cottage at the west end of the lake.
6. Whose house is the one with the wall made of stones?
7. "Mind your *p*'s and *q*'s," my grandmother used to warn me, but I'm sure the phrase wasn't hers originally.
8. Most of the M.P.'s from our province are members of the governing party.
9. correct (*£s, ¶s, and ®s also acceptable*)
10. My Oldsmobile's body is rusty, but its engine runs like new.

Exercise 19.5

1. Mona's habit of dotting her *i*'s with happy faces failed to impress her employers.
2. It's been a long while since I last went bowling, but my friends say that bowling's time has come.
3. Correcting these sentences is more fun than a trip to Disneyland, isn't it?
4. Isn't it too bad that Malik's car's muffler fell off on the way to his wedding?
5. "I'll show you mine if you show me yours," squealed Sergei, clutching his stamp collection to his chest and wiggling his ears enthusiastically.
6. We're all going to the party on New Year's Eve at eight o'clock in the evening.
7. Who's going to believe that's how a gentleman's supposed to act?
8. Hers were fond memories of Victoria's beautiful gardens.
9. Oh, a sailor's life's the life for me.
10. "You're not going anywhere for awhile," he said, "because your car battery's dead and I've got to finish putting this engine back together."

Exercise 19.6

1. This year's hockey season started earlier than last year's.
2. If you're not listening, you can't know what we're planning to do.

3. The flight to Toronto was nearly forty-five minutes late, but at least Aaron's baggage was transferred automatically.
4. He'll try to tell you what you should and shouldn't do, but don't overestimate his wisdom.
5. The cat licked its paws carefully before jumping onto Bess's lap.
6. Their car wouldn't start, so they're going to drive with their neighbours.
7. Studies have shown that professors' jobs are less boring than most.
8. Once we're finished here, let's leave what's left for tomorrow.
9. It's well known that theirs is faster than ours.
10. I should've loaned her ours because she couldn't get yours out of the box.

Exercise 20.1

1. Wordsworth's lyric about being surprised by joy appears in many school readers.
2. "Bang! You're Dead!" shouted wee Tommy, while Aunty Bea felt her angina pectoris returning like a bullet in her chest.
3. "See ya, Daddy," said the toddler sadly as Mr. Slominski left for Kamloops.
4. "Dare I intrude?" Mr. Schiller asked plaintively.
5. "Don't start your 'Dare I intrude?' routine," Bert replied, offering him a chair.
6. Rosa told us that you are going to Geneva this winter.
7. Ross's "The Painted Door" is one of the most memorable short stories I can remember.
8. The poem "Death of a Young Son by Drowning" from Margaret Atwood's collection *The Journals of Susanna Moodie* ends with the memorable simile, "I planted him in this country / like a flag."
9. According to most guides to writing, a good writer does not overuse quotation marks.
10. Roland repeated, as if we hadn't heard him the first time, "The greatest poem of the twentieth century is Pound's 'In a Station of the Metro' because it takes so little time to read."

Exercise 20.2

1. "Me go out with André?" exclaimed Monique. "That wimp! That bore! That drip! And besides that, he hasn't asked me."
2. correct
3. In his *Life of Samuel Johnson*, James Boswell quotes Johnson on writing for pay: "No man but a blockhead ever wrote except for money."
4. correct
5. Professor Dooley was obsessed with the idea that "The Fall of the House of Usher" was symbolically about autumn.
6. As the spelling suggests, The Beatles were not thinking of insects when they chose a name for their musical group.

7. Having failed to borrow a spare tire for his crippled truck, Danny was heard to remark that it was a long road that had no turning.
8. "I've been trying to finish *War and Peace* since I was fourteen," confessed Jason.
9. Professor Edwards was thrilled when his article "The Physical Source of Bunyan's Slough" appeared in the journal *Studies in Literary Geography*.
10. "Stand up and be counted," Ms. Rousseau commanded the kindergarten class.

Exercise 20.3

1. "Let's get down to the nitty-gritty issues and put all the hollow rhetoric aside," suggested the head negotiator for the union.
2. Tennyson depicts Ulysses in age as one "Made weak by time and fate, but strong in will."
3. Moby Dick is not actually the main character of Melville's novel *Moby Dick*.
4. correct
5. Because it is so often anthologized, particularly in school readers, "David" is probably Earle Birney's best-known poem.
6. correct (or "Litotes")
7. "Never a borrower or a lender be," said Aunt Mattie, who had a proverb ready for every occasion.
8. Bookstore managers report that the Bible is the most frequently stolen book.
9. "It would seem that Birney's poem 'The Bear on the Delhi Road' is as much about men as bears," remarked Ramesh gravely.
10. "I'll have three litres of two-percent and a half litre of cream for Tabby," Mrs. Sanchez told the cow.

Exercise 21.1

1. The captain shouted excitedly from the upper deck, "Abandon ship! Women and children first! Then man the lifeboats!"
2. Mrs. Perrier called to inquire how we were getting along with digging our well.
3. Is it true that a virtual university is offering a three-month correspondence course leading to a Ph.D.?
4. The same organization—can you believe it?—will make you a saint for $99.95.
5. "Can you really be serious?" she asked.
6. "When I was in junior high," Mabel reminisced, "we had dances in the gym, and I was kissed for the first time while slow dancing on the foul line."
7. Alas, the exclamation point is all too often overworked.
8. Dr. Beluga had sacrificed his chance to be a pool shark in order to become an M.D.

9. The road to the climber's hut on Orizaba, Mexico's highest mountain, runs to a point over three hundred metres (?) higher than the highest mountain in the Canadian Rockies.
10. "Are we feeling better today?" crooned the physician, in his best bedside manner.

Exercise 21.2

1. The participants in the local "flab wars" were The Fit Family Emporium, Club Gristle, The God and Goddess, and The Burning Bod.
2. We'll have to be up with the sun because the bus leaves at 6:45 A.M.
3. correct
4. The scouts were filled with anticipation when they saw the sign that said only twelve kilometres more to Athabasca Pass.
5. Just think what the Romans managed to achieve in the line of decadence without disco, without punk, and without video games.
6. Helena has several ambitions: to run a marathon, to become a trial lawyer, to live somewhere where it never snows, and to remain healthy until she is one hundred.
7. Rev. McKinley based his sermon on Hebrews 11:3: "By faith we understand that the world was created by the word of God, so that what is seen was made out of things which do not appear."
8. correct
9. correct
10. Our flight passed over various places that I had never seen from the ground, such as Saskatoon, Winnipeg, and Owen Sound.

Exercise 21.3

1. If a person wants to write well—poetry, fiction, or just correspondence—that person must take the time to practise writing.
2. The audience—producers, top-name performers, leading critics— gave the performers a standing ovation.
3. Science and mathematics are required of all engineering students, while English—though not considered a liability in the profession—is optional.
4. Can't act, can't sing, can't dance—are you sure you belong in show business?
5. correct
6. When one is flying at 12,000 metres, Lake Superior looks like an ocean—but, then, so does the land around it.
7. Canada has at least one sport—hockey—in which it leads the world.
8. Antique farm equipment, old cars, broken appliances, rolls of wire, and tall, grasping weeds—all these made traversing their yard an adventure.
9. correct

10. A study of comparative interest in various jobs has shown—not too surprisingly—that workers on assembly lines find their jobs boring.

Exercise 21.4

1. High altitude pulmonary edema (often abbreviated HAPE), which is essentially fluid in the air cells of the lungs, is the most dangerous kind of altitude sickness.
2. According to Dr. James A. Wilkerson's *Medicine for Mountaineering*, the chances of an adult getting high altitude pulmonary edema after ascending quickly to 3,700 metres (12,000 feet) is about one in 200 (0.5 percent).
3. Symptoms include tiredness, coughing, shortness of breath, fast heartbeat, and bubbling sounds (rales) in the lungs.
4. "O chestnut tree, great-rooted blossomer, / Are you the leaf, the blossom, or the bole [trunk]?" asks Yeats, considering process and change in "Among School Children."
5. "Thus Constance [sic] does make cowards of us all . . ." proclaimed the nervous Hamlet and then froze.
6. When a student attempted to answer an examination question on Coleridge's "The Rime of the Ancient Mariner" without having read the poem, he/she made the mistake of saying, "They then hung Albert Ross [sic] around the mariner's neck."
7. "I desire those politicians who dislike my overture . . . that they will first ask the parents of these mortals whether they would not at this day think it a great happiness to have been sold for food at a year old in the manner I prescribe, and thereby have avoided such a perpetual scene of misfortunes as they have since gone through by the oppression of landlords," writes Swift near the end of "A Modest Proposal."
8. "The advantages of deep-breathing exercises cannot be overstressed. . . . Consciously increasing the ratio of breaths to steps is also well worthwhile," writes one authority on altitude sickness.
9. correct
10. An aged thrush, frail, gaunt, and small,

    . . . .

    Had chosen thus to fling his soul

    Upon the growing gloom.

    Thomas Hardy, "The Darkling Thrush"

Exercise 21.5

1. "Our line of winter wear has been very warmly received (no pun intended)," boasted the manufacturer.
2. "Hurry!" she said. "The sun has been up for hours, and the others have been gone since first light."

3. Black eyes sparkling, hair carefully washed and combed, teeth as clean as crunching dog biscuits could make them, his little tail poised to wag cutely at the slightest provocation—Snooky entered the audition knowing he was the best dog he could be.
4. "Who's cooking breakfast this morning?" came the muffled question from Brad's sleeping bag.
5. "What a beautiful day," exclaimed Vincenzo. "The sky stretches all the way round the horizon."
6. People who normally live at high altitude may develop high altitude pulmonary edema if they descend to a much lower level for one or two weeks (or, of course, more) and then ascend quickly to high altitude.
7. Lindsay, like her parents, came to regard the bowling alley as her home away from home: she was really into bowling.
8. As the summer wore on, Orville found he was asking himself again and again whether being a lifeguard in a wading pool was the challenging occupation he had hoped it would be.
9. "I have been one acquainted with the night," begins one of Robert Frost's bleaker and more tightly written poems.
10. I hadn't paid for my trip in advance, so I was not greatly disturbed to find that my travel agent had taken an unscheduled trip of her own to some unspecified destination in South America.

Exercise 21.6

1. correct
2. Niggard, skinflint, lickpenny, moneygrubber, tightwad—such names could not distract Mr. Biggs from his ambition to make himself the richest man in the business.
3. correct
4. "You don't think I look too bright, do you?" said Louis, referring, of course, to his new yellow sport coat.
5. When driving in winter, you will be wise to carry emergency supplies: a tool kit, basic replacement parts, emergency candles, something sweet to eat, extra clothing, and a cell phone.
6. After his release from prison, Mugsie found himself in brisk demand on the talk-show circuit and in lecture halls.
7. Carmine reported that his Uncle Guido had spent his first day home from his round-the-world, solo voyage reading the personals columns in the local papers and mumbling to himself.
8. Ling had to run to get to her psych class by 2:30 P.M.
9. Remember this: the lines in the middle of the road are yellow, and the ones on the sides are white.
10. Oddly, the plants that grew best in the garden were the weeds.

Exercise 22.1

1. tobacco
2. tomatoes
3. likelihood
4. development
5. disagreement
6. correct
7. correct
8. a yoke of oxen
9. re-educate
10. resemblance
11. self-satisfied
12. in his forties
13. innocence
14. laboratory
15. government

Exercise 22.2

1. argument
2. pastime
3. architecture
4. achievement
5. both mothers-in-law
6. seven-year itch
7. quizzes
8. correct
9. criteria
10. a real eye-opener
11. heifer
12. vacuum
13. ex-landlord
14. happier
15. calendar

Exercise 22.3

1. self-
   explanatory
2. correct
3. sister-
   in-law
4. obey
5. objec-
   tively
   OR objectively
6. sit-
   ting
7. paral-
   lel
8. wood-
   pecker
   OR woodpecker
9. pass-
   ing
10. mayor-elect

Exercise 22.4

1. "Before dying," the famous detective observed, "the count must have placed the message in the envelope."
2. Both the print and broadcast media co-operated to expose the corruption in the sewer and water department.
3. A lot of leaves have been turned on the calendar since I saw you last.
4. The self-study was aimed at reducing office expenses to manageable levels.
5. After ten prolific years as a playwright, O'Malley quit and remained quiet for quite a few years.
6. The temperature in Calgary is undoubtedly colder than that of St. John's in winter, but, then, it's usually hotter in summer.
7. Mr. Blair would have accepted the appointment except for the problems he anticipated in moving his family overseas.
8. Debbie must have made it to shore since we found her life preserver and her coat in the same place.
9. The headmaster of the school received a letter of censure from a group of concerned parents who felt the books he had allowed in the school library were undermining the morals of their children.
10. Guerrilla warfare certainly would have been the answer to their problem, but they had nobody to train the troops.

Exercise 23.1

1. Dalhousie University
2. Mrs. Tymchuk, the mayor
3. Freudianism
4. Saskatchewan Roughriders football team
5. the Arctic Circle
6. Grey Cup
7. Greenland whale
8. Socratic method
9. correct
10. the Big Dipper
11. correct
12. Morse code
13. correct
14. German measles
15. St. Francis

Exercise 23.2

1. Russian Orthodox Church
2. malaria
3. UNICEF

4. Girl Guides of Canada
5. Halley's comet
6. April Fools' Day
7. Imperial Order Daughters of the Empire
8. correct
9. Corner Brook, Newfoundland
10. the Maritimes
11. Richards' *Hope in the Desperate Hour*
12. Memorial Park
13. correct
14. Saint John River
15. Premier Campbell

Exercise 23.3

1. "I tell you, I have seen the Flying Dutchman with my own two eyes," shouted Captain Jacobson.
2. "Oh, but I wish I were going to be here to hear the Nobel Prize winner speak," exclaimed Bertrand.
3. The children in the Sunday school did not have complete Bibles, just the New Testament and Psalms.
4. Yi-Su intends to go to graduate school to get her doctorate.
5. She is transferring from Simon Fraser University to a university in Toronto.
6. While at Loon Lake, they caught six trout and a smallmouth bass.
7. One of the characters in the medieval morality play *Everyman* is Good Deeds.
8. Professor Kotsopoulos, my favourite English professor, does not have a Ph.D.
9. Andy will start work driving a Brink's truck as soon as he finishes school in the spring.
10. Evergreen Books on the south side of the boulevard near the subway station has good deals on encyclopedias.

Exercise 24.1

1. Even educated native speakers of English will sometimes confuse forms of lay and lie.
2. Starting the day with CTV's Canada AM has become almost a tradition at our house.
3. Many of the more colourful Maritime place names, such as Passamaquoddy and Nepisiguit, are derived from Micmac and Malecite words.
4. One man's de rigueur is another's hoity-toity.
5. Vis-à-vis what?

6. The phrase de profundis—out of the depths—is taken from the opening of the Latin version of Psalm 130.
7. De Profundis is also the title of a prose apologia written by Oscar Wilde in prison.
8. Her favourite fictional subject was the faux pas of the nouveau riche.
9. King Lear is one of Shakespeare's best tragedies.
10. "Bon appétit," Captain Patch was heard to remark while feeding the piranhas.

Exercise 24.2

1. Some people prefer to cross their 7's to avoid having them mistaken for 1's.
2. Others find that a crossed 7 looks too much like a 4.
3. C'est la vie!
4. Alden Nowlan's hilarious story "Miracle at Indian River" appears in a collection also called Miracle at Indian River.
5. Of all his stories, it is perhaps the most strikingly a tour de force.
6. Nowlan had been a reporter for the Observer in Hartland, New Brunswick, the general area where the story is set, and he knew his subjects well.
7. correct
8. The television episodes of Star Trek, along with the movies based on the series, have made the starship Enterprise as famous as any real spacecraft.
9. The Spanish word junta, formerly pronounced with an h, has now become Anglicized to the point where it can also be pronounced with a j.
10. The coup d'état was a fait accompli, and the president was being held incommunicado.

Exercise 25.1

1. at 21 Athabasca Avenue, Devon, Alberta ✔
2. AIDS ✔
3. 1/2 of the way home ✕
4. seventy-three years old ✔
5. "4 good reasons come to mind," said Mr. Weiner. ✕
6. Grade 2 ✕
7. after receiving his B. Comm. ✕
8. a Sr. partner in the firm ✕
9. about 630 B.C. ✔
10. RCMP ✔
11. Chas. Irwin ✕
12. won two million dollars ✔

13. Phase 3 ✔
14. CBC ✔
15. June 2nd, 2002 ✕

Exercise 25.2

1. N.B. Power ✔
2. in Prof. Mayberry's office ✕
3. over three million copies in print ✔
4. Highway 2 ✔
5. The Rev. had a bad cold for the memorial service. ✕
6. attendance of three thousand, two hundred, and sixty-one ✕
7. nine A.M. ✕
8. St. Lawrence River ✔
9. working 6 days a week ✕
10. The decision finally came down to Psych. 201 or Phil. 310. ✕
11. The retired Gen. liked to be called by his military title. ✕
12. Ms. B.N. Ramsingh, B.Ed., et al. ✔
13. next Thurs. ✕
14. the second chapt. of the text ✕
15. A.D. Lam, master of arts ✕

Proofreading Marks

Proofreading mark	Draft copy	Final copy
Align horizontally	TO: Rick Munoz	TO: Rick Munoz
Align vertically	166.32 132.45	166.32 132.45
Capitalize	Coca-cola runs on ms-dos	Coca-Cola runs on MS-DOS
Close up space	meeting at 3 p. m.	meeting at 3 p.m.
Centre	Recommendations	Recommendations
Delete	in my final judgement	in my judgment
Insert apostrophe	our companys product	our company's product
Insert comma	you will of course	you will, of course,
Insert semicolon	value therefore, we feel	value; therefore, we feel
Insert hyphen	tax free income	tax-free income
Insert period	Ms Holly Hines	Ms. Holly Hines
Insert quotation mark	shareholders receive a bonus	shareholders receive a "bonus"
Insert space	wordprocessing program	word processing program
Lowercase (remove capitals)	the Vice-President HUMAN RESOURCES	the vice-president Human Resources
Move to left	I. Labour costs	I. Labour costs
Move to right	A. Findings of study	A. Findings of study
Spell out	aimed at 2 depts	aimed at two departments
Start new paragraph	Keep the screen height at eye level.	Keep the screen height at eye level.
Stet (don't delete)	officials talked openly	officials talked openly
Transpose	accounts recievable	accounts receivable
Use boldface	Conclusions	**Conclusions**
Use italics	The Perfect Résumé	*The Perfect Résumé*
Start new line	Globex, 23 Acorn Lane	Globex 23 Acorn Lane
Run lines together	Invoice No. 122059	Invoice No. 122059

Notes